THE WORLD'S BEST
STORAGE & SHELVING PROJECTS

BEST OF POPULAR WOODWORKING MAGAZINE

**POPULAR
WOODWORKING
BOOKS**

CINCINNATI, OHIO
www.popularwoodworking.com

READ THIS IMPORTANT SAFETY NOTICE

To prevent accidents, keep safety in mind while you work. The tool guards in some photos have been removed for clarity. Always use the safety guards installed on power equipment; they are for your protection. When working on power equipment, keep fingers away from saw blades, wear safety goggles to prevent injuries from flying wood chips and sawdust, wear headphones to protect your hearing and consider installing a dust vacuum to reduce the amount of airborne sawdust in your woodshop. Don't wear loose clothing, such as neckties or shirts with loose sleeves, or jewelry, such as rings, necklaces or bracelets, when working on power equipment. Tie back long hair to prevent it from getting caught in your equipment. People who are sensitive to certain chemicals should check the chemical content of any product before using it. The authors and editors who compiled this book have tried to make the contents as accurate and correct as possible. Plans, illustrations, photographs and text have been carefully checked. All instructions, plans and projects should be carefully read, studied and understood before beginning construction. Due to the variability of local conditions, construction materials, skill levels, etc., neither the author nor Popular Woodworking Books assumes any responsibility for any accidents, injuries, damages or other losses incurred resulting from the material presented in this book. Prices listed for supplies and equipment were current at the time of publication and are subject to change. Glass shelving should have all edges polished and must be tempered. Untempered glass shelves may shatter and can cause serious bodily injury. Tempered shelves are very strong and if they break will just crumble, minimizing personal injury.

METRIC CONVERSION CHART

TO CONVERT	TO	MULTIPLY BY
Inches	Centimeters	2.54
Centimeters	Inches	0.4
Feet	Centimeters	30.5
Centimeters	Feet	0.03
Yards	Meters	0.9
Meters	Yards	1.1
Sq. Inches	Sq. Centimeters	6.45
Sq. Centimeters	Sq. Inches	0.16
Sq. Feet	Sq. Meters	0.09
Sq. Meters	Sq. Feet	10.8
Sq. Yards	Sq. Meters	0.8
Sq. Meters	Sq. Yards	1.2
Pounds	Kilograms	0.45
Kilograms	Pounds	2.2
Ounces	Grams	28.3
Grams	Ounces	0.035

The World's Best Storage & Shelving Projects. Copyright © 2002 by Popular Woodworking Books. Manufactured in China. All rights reserved. No part of this book may be reproduced in any form or by any electronic or mechanical means including information storage and retrieval systems without permission in writing from the publisher, except by a reviewer, who may quote brief passages in a review. Published by Popular Woodworking Books, an imprint of F&W Publications, Inc., 4700 East Galbraith Road, Cincinnati, Ohio, 45236. First edition.

Visit our Web site at www.popularwoodworking.com for more information and resources for woodworkers.

Other fine Popular Woodworking Books are available from your local bookstore or direct from the publisher.

06   05   04   03   5   4   3   2

Library of Congress Cataloging-in-Publication Data
The world's best storage & shelving projects : 23projects for your home / from the editors of Popular woodworking.
      p. cm.
      ISBN 1-55870-639-9
1. Cabinetwork--Amateurs' manuals. 2. Shelving (Furniture)--Amateurs' manuals. 3. Storage in the home--Amateurs' manuals. I. Title: World's best shelving projects. II. Popular woodworking.

TT197 .W85 2002
684.1'6--dc21
2002066248

Editor: Jim Stack
Associate Editor: Jennifer Ziegler
Designer: Brian Roeth
Layout Artist: Kathy Gardner
Lead photography by Al Parrish
Step-by-step photography by Popular Woodworking staff
Illustrations by John W. Hutchinson, Jim Stuard and Jim Stack
Production coordinated by Mark Griffin

CREDITS
Staff of *Popular Woodworking* magazine
  Christopher Schwarz, Senior Editor: Asian Bedside Table
  Steve Shanesy, Editor and Publisher:Barrister Bookcases, Tall Pine Clock, Boating Bookshelf
  David Thiel, Senior Editor: Basic Bookcases, Built-In Bookcases, Shaker Firewood Box, Hanging China Cupboard, Storage & Assembly Bench, European Telephone Console
Contributors
  Wendy Dunning: Apothecary Cabinet
  Glen Huey: Pennsylvania Spice Box, Inlay Door with a Router
  Mag Ruffman: Tank Heaven
  Troy Sexton: What You Must Know About Shelving (Cherry Shelving Units), Traditional Entertainment Center, Country Dry Sink, Shaker Storage Cabinet
  Jim Stuard, Former Associate Editor: Shaker Hanging Shelf, All-In-One Cabinet for the Small Shop, Modern Occassional Table
  Rick Peters: Craftsman Wall Shelf
  Michel Theriault: Stacking Storage Boxes
PENNSYLVANIA SPICE BOX & INLAY DOOR WITH A ROUTER: © 2002 by Glen Huey. All rights reserved. Originally appeared in December 2001 and February 2002 *Popular Woodworking* magazine.
TANK HEAVEN: © 2002 by Mag Ruffman. All rights reserved. Originally appeared in February 2002 *Popular Woodworking* magazine.
WHAT YOU MUST KNOW ABOUT SHELVING: © 2002 by Troy Sexton. All rights reserved. Originally appeared in August 2000 *Popular Woodworking* magazine.
TRADITIONAL ENTERTAINMENT CENTER: © 2002 by Troy Sexton. All rights reserved. Originally appeared in June 2001 *Popular Woodworking* magazine.
COUNTRY DRY SINK: © 2001 by Troy Sexton. All rights reserved. Originally appeared in August 2001 *Popular Woodworking* magazine.
CRAFTSMAN WALL SHELF: © 2002 by Rick Peters. All rights reserved. Originally appeared in December 2001 *Popular Woodworking* magazine.
STACKING STORAGE BOXES: © 2002 by Michel Theriault. All rights reserved. Originally appeared in September 1998 *Popular Woodworking* magazine.
SHAKER STORAGE CABINET: © 2002 by Troy Sexton. All rights reserved. Originally appeared in April 2002 *Popular Woodworking* magazine.

introduction

We've all heard the saying, "Everything has a place and everything in its place" ... or something to that effect. Everyone has things – things that need a place to rest and to be accessible when they are wanted or needed.

The editors and contributing editors of *Popular Woodworking* magazine have almost 200 years of experience among them. They have made mistakes and learned the right way to build projects correctly the first time.

The projects in this book offer something for everyone (and everything!). From the bathroom to the bedroom, the den to the workshop, basic shelving projects to high-end bookcases, it's all here! We have gathered together the most popular and practical storage and shelving projects from the pages of *Popular Woodworking* magazine into one concise book.

There are a wide range of projects to choose from in this book. It is our goal to provide you, the reader and woodworker, the best range of projects for every skill level, storage and shelving need. Each of the projects presented has very clear text, photos, technical drawings and cutting lists – everything needed to build these projects easily and correctly the first time!

So, as we say here at Popular Woodworking, "Let's start making some sawdust!"

table of contents

cherry
shelving units

Learn the simple but important rules to building sturdy shelves. Then build this handsome bookcase – or adapt the design using these easy-to-learn standards.

Building a set of shelves for muddy boots or a Chippendale secretary seems deceptively simple. First you install a horizontal surface between two sides. Then you load up your newly built shelf with Wellingtons or glass kitty cats, stand back and admire your work.

One day you grow weary of the kitties and decide to put encyclopedias on your shelf. The shelf sags; the books don't fit under the shelf above, and the books' spines hang over the front edge. You wish you had used a more rigid material and adjustable shelf pins so you could change your shelves to fit your needs.

Shelves, as you might have guessed, are not as simple as they appear. That's not to say they're hard to build. It's just that there's a whole set of rules that applies to properly designed bookshelves and display shelves, which ensures that they will hold a wide variety of common objects.

This shelving unit is the perfect tutorial for etching these rules into your brain. You'll see how I followed the rules to design this project, and you'll get a down-and-dirty lesson in how to build shelving units that are quick, easy, rock solid and good-looking.

Here are a couple rules of thumb when you're putting your design on paper. It's accepted practice to build your cabinets in 3" increments. For example, the side units are 24" wide. If I wanted to make them wider, I'd jump to 27", then 30". Another rule of thumb is that whenever a cabinet is 42" or wider it needs a vertical support in the center. My cabinets are shorter than that, so that was no problem for me.

Where to Begin: Face First

This large wall unit is essentially six plywood boxes with solid wood face frames on front. The part of the back that is visible behind the shelves is solid wood. The back behind the doors is plywood.

When building shelves, it's tempting to begin with the case because it goes together really fast. Resist this temptation. Begin your project by building the solid wood face frames. Your entire project is based on your face frame, so if you have a problem with your design, or how you milled your parts, you're most likely to find out about it when you build the face frame. And I'd rather throw away a skinny piece of solid wood than a sheet of plywood.

I make my face frames using ¾" material and mortise-and-tenon construction. First I cut my tenons on the rails, then I use those to lay out my mortises on my stiles. When working with ¾" material, I always make my tenons ⅜" thick and 1" long. Usually I cut a ½" shoulder on the width of the tenon, but if the stock is narrow (less than 3") I'll use a ¼" shoulder. I cut my tenons on my table saw using a dado stack.

I now lay out my mortises using the tenons. Cut the mortises — I use a hollow-chisel mortiser — about $1\frac{1}{16}$" deep so the tenon won't bottom out in the mortise. Put glue in the mortises, clamp and set the frames aside.

cherry shelving units **inches**

CENTER CASE, UPPER UNIT

No.	Item	Dimensions T W L	Mat.
1	Bot rail	¾ x 1½ x 33	P
1	Top rail	¾ x 4 x 33	P
2	Stiles	¾ x 4¾ x 50	P
1	Top	¾ x 16¾ x 39½	Ply
3	Adj shelves*	¾ x 16 x 38¾	Ply
1	Bottom	¾ x 16¾ x 39½	Ply
2	Sides	¾ x 17¼ x 50	Ply
2	Columns	1 x 3 x 50	P
	Back	½ x 39½ x 50	P

SIDE CASE, ONE UPPER UNIT

No.	Item	Dimensions T W L	Mat.
1	Bot rail	¾ x 1½ x 21	P
1	Top rail	¾ x 4 x 21	P
1	Int. stile	¾ x 2⅝ x 50	P
1	Ext. stile	¾ x 2½ x 50	P
1	Top	¾ x 12¾ x 23	Ply
3	Adj shelves*	¾ x 12 x 22¼	Ply
1	Bottom	¾ x 12¾ x 23	Ply
2	Sides	¾ x 13¼ x 50	Ply
	Back	½ x 23 x 50	P

CENTER CASE, LOWER UNIT

No.	Item	Dimensions T W L	Mat.
1	Top rail	¾ x 1½ x 33	P
1	Bot rail	¾ x 5 x 33	P
2	Stiles	¾ x 4¾ x 30	P
1	Bot	¾ x 16¾ x 39½	Ply
1	Adj shelf*	¾ x 16 x 38¾	Ply
1	Top rail	¾ x 1½ x 39	P
2	Sides	¾ x 17¼ x 30	Ply
2	Columns	1 x 3 x 30	P
	Back	¼ x 39½ x 26¼	Ply

SIDE CASE, ONE LOWER UNIT

No.	Item	Dimensions T W L	Mat.
1	Top rail	¾ x 1½ x 21	P
1	Bot rail	¾ x 5 x 21	P
1	Int. stile	¾ x 2⅝ x 30	P
1	Ext. stile	¾ x 2½ x 30	P
1	Bot	¾ x 12¾ x 23	Ply
1	Adj shelf*	¾ x 12 x 22¼	Ply
1	Top rail	¾ x 1½ x 22½	P
2	Sides	¾ x 13¼ x 30	Ply
	Back	¼ x 23 x 26¼	Ply

ONE CENTER UNIT DOOR

No.	Item	Dimensions T W L	Mat.
2	Rails	¾ x 2½ x 12½	P
2	Stiles	¾ x 2½ x 23½	P
1	Panel	⅝ x 11 x 19	P

ONE SIDE UNIT DOOR

No.	Item	Dimensions T W L	Mat.
2	Rails	¾ x 2½ x 16	P
2	Stiles	¾ x 2½ x 23½	P
1	Panel	⅝ x 14½ x 19	P

* width includes dropped edge

P=Cherry • Ply=Cherry ply

Drill your shelf pin holes before you assemble your case. I like to put mine on 1" or 2" centers. Depending on what you're going to put on your shelves, you might not need that many holes.

KEEP YOUR SHELVES FROM SAGGING

You don't want your shelves to sag, yet you don't want to waste materials by overbuilding them either. In general, here are the guidelines for how long shelves can be before they start to sag, according to the Architectural Woodwork Institute. Typical shelves vary from 8" deep to 12" deep.

MATERIAL	MAX SPAN ($^3/_4$" mat.)	MAX SPAN ($1^1/_{16}$" mat.)
Solid wood	36"	48"
Veneer-core ply	36"	48"
Medium density fiberboard	32"	42"

Of course, some woods and manufactured wood products are stronger than others. The following chart shows how much weight it takes to make a 12"-wide shelf bend $^1/_4$" across a 36" span and a 48" span. As you can see below, solid wood makes the strongest shelves, followed by a manufactured shelf with a solid wood edge that's wider than the plywood is thick (commonly referred to as a "dropped" edge). This is the shelf I used for the project.

SHELF MATERIAL	36" SPAN	48" SPAN
Yellow poplar	284 lbs.	117 lbs.
Hard maple & red oak	313	232
Birch	348	146
MDF	87	38
Birch veneer-core ply	129	54
Birch veneer MDF	109	46
MDF with .05" thick laminate	205	87
MDF with $^1/_8$" wood edge	79	33
MDF with $^3/_4$" wood edge	90	38
MDF with $^3/_4$" x $1^1/_2$" wood edge, dropped	241	107

Source: Architectural Woodwork Institute, Department of Wood Science, Division of Forestry at West Virginia University

Doors

Build the doors the same way you built the face frames, with one exception. You'll need to cut a $^3/_8$" × $^3/_8$" groove on the rails and stiles for the solid wood panel. That also means you'll need to cut haunches on your tenons to fit into the grooves.

With raised panels I allow a $^1/_8$" gap on each side so the panel can expand and contract in the groove. To "raise" the panel, first cut the approximate angle on the panel's edge using your table saw. Then use an 8° raised-panel cutter in your router to raise the panel. This way you'll only need to make one pass on your router table. Sand the panel, assemble the doors, then sand the rest of the door. Peg the tenons, cut the pegs $^1/_{16}$" proud and sand them smooth but not flush to the doors.

Attach the pulls and fit your doors so there's a $^1/_{16}$" gap all around. I use Amerock adjustable non-mortise hinges. These hinges are pricey (about $3 each) but they are worth every penny because they are simple to install and are adjustable.

COMMON SIZES OF STUFF YOU PUT ON A SHELF

When building shelves for a specific purpose, say, for an entertainment center, you need to plan around the standard sizes of objects. Use these handy dimensions to figure out your shelf opening heights and depths.

OBJECT	DEPTH X HEIGHT
Paperbacks	$4^1/_4$" x $6^7/_8$"
Hardbacks	7" x $9^1/_2$"
Textbooks	9" x 11"
Vinyl LPs	$12^3/_8$" x $12^3/_8$"
Compact discs	$5^1/_2$" x 5"
Cassettes	$2^3/_4$" x $4^1/_4$"
DVDs	$5^1/_2$" x $7^1/_2$"
VHS tapes	$4^1/_8$" x $7^1/_2$"

Back and Shelves

I used a shiplapped and beaded $^1/_2$"-thick back on the top part of the case, and a plywood back on the lower section. Cut your $^1/_4$" × $^1/_2$" shiplaps, then cut the bead on the edge using a $^1/_4$" beading bit in your router. Fit the back, being sure to leave space for seasonal expansion and contraction. Don't nail the back in place until after finishing. Cut your shelves from plywood, nail the moulding to it, then sand the shelves.

Finishing

I used a clear finish on this piece, sanding between coats with 3M sanding sponges (fine grit). Nothing gets into moulding and raised panels better. When everything's dry, nail your back pieces in place and hang your doors.

Supplies

Rockler • 800-279-4441, or www.rockler.com
Non-mortising hinges - #31300

Horton Brasses Inc. • 800-754-9127, or www.horton-brasses.com
Knobs - #K-12 w/MSF (machine screw fitting)

basic **bookcases**

When it comes to furniture projects, there isn't an easier place to start than bookcases. As far as practical furniture goes, you'll be amazed by what can be stored in them.

The two bookcases offered here are made of solid oak, edge-glued to reach finished width. Use dadoes, glue and finish nails for joints. All dadoes are through-dadoes except for those in the top which are stopped $^3/_8$" from the front edge.

A $^3/_8$" × $^3/_8$" through-rabbet runs on the inside back edge of all the sides. A stopped rabbet runs on the inside back edge of each top.

Use a template to locate the shelf pins, which are drilled to provide equal spaces. Drill extra holes 1" up and 1" down from the equidistant holes for adjustable spacing.

You can finish these bookcases with a few coats of clear satin lacquer. But if natural color or lacquer isn't your first choice, you can choose from any number of stain options or clear topcoats.

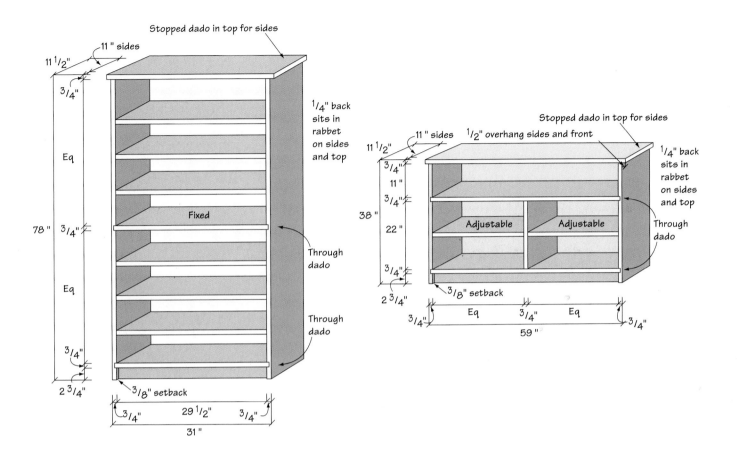

No.	Item	Dimensions T W L	Material
LOW BOOKCASE			
1	Top	$3/4 \times 11^{1}/_{2} \times 60$	Solid Oak
2	Sides	$3/4 \times 11 \times 37^{5}/_{8}$	Solid Oak
2	Bot/Shelf	$3/4 \times 10^{5}/_{8} \times 58^{1}/_{4}$	Solid Oak
1	Center	$3/4 \times 10^{5}/_{8} \times 22^{3}/_{4}$	Solid Oak
1	Kick	$3/4 \times 2^{3}/_{4} \times 57^{1}/_{2}$	Solid Oak
2	Shelves	$3/4 \times 10^{1}/_{2} \times 28^{3}/_{8}$	Solid Oak
1	Back	$1/4 \times 34^{7}/_{8} \times 58^{1}/_{4}$	Oak Ply
TALL BOOKCASE			
1	Top	$3/4 \times 11^{1}/_{2} \times 32$	Solid Oak
2	Sides	$3/4 \times 11 \times 77^{5}/_{8}$	Solid Oak
2	Bot/Shelf	$3/4 \times 10^{5}/_{8} \times 30^{1}/_{4}$	Solid Oak
1	Kick	$3/4 \times 2^{3}/_{4} \times 29^{1}/_{2}$	Solid Oak
6	Shelves	$3/4 \times 10^{1}/_{2} \times 29^{1}/_{2}$	Solid Oak
1	Back	$1/4 \times 30^{3}/_{4} \times 74^{7}/_{8}$	Oak Ply

basic bookcases **inches**

basic bookcases **millimeters**

No.	Item	Dimensions T W L	Material
LOW BOOKCASE			
1	Top	$19 \times 292 \times 1524$	Solid Oak
2	Sides	$19 \times 279 \times 956$	Solid Oak
2	Bot/Shelf	$19 \times 270 \times 1479$	Solid Oak
1	Center	$19 \times 270 \times 579$	Solid Oak
1	Kick	$19 \times 70 \times 1461$	Solid Oak
2	Shelves	$19 \times 267 \times 721$	Solid Oak
1	Back	$6 \times 886 \times 1479$	Oak Ply
TALL BOOKCASE			
1	Top	$19 \times 292 \times 813$	Solid Oak
2	Sides	$19 \times 279 \times 1972$	Solid Oak
2	Bot/Shelf	$19 \times 270 \times 768$	Solid Oak
1	Kick	$19 \times 70 \times 750$	Solid Oak
6	Shelves	$19 \times 267 \times 750$	Solid Oak
1	Back	$6 \times 768 \times 1902$	Oak Ply

tank
heaven

End bathroom clutter and elude
the annoying plop of destiny.

At least once a year I knock something off the bathroom counter, right into the toilet. It's usually a highly non-disposable item, like my favorite hairbrush. There follows the humbling act of fishing the item out of the bowl. Then the challenge of cleaning it. The dishwasher is tempting, unless you live with nosy people who'd want to know why your hairbrush is in the cutlery rack on sani-cycle.

I don't blame myself for knocking stuff into the toilet because it's society's fault. In the old days, a single bar of soap served as shampoo, shaving foam, skin care regimen and deodorant. Washing was a once-a-week proposition. People smelled a bit, but they spent most of the day behind a horse who didn't seem to mind. Folks got cleaned up on Saturday night to prepare for the next morning, when being crammed into a church pew was the social event of the week.

In contrast, today's society is a teeming 24/7 press of bodies, with people crushed together in buses, offices, restaurants and movie theaters. We don't do much of anything alone, and we can't afford to smell bad.

And here's my point: There just isn't adequate surface area in modern bathrooms to contain all the tools families require for personal grooming. Many families have an arsenal of products perched around the sink, the edges of the tub and atop the toilet tank.

Society gave us this clutter, but God gave us elbows. So on a bad day one of those personal grooming products is going for a swim.

My answer to society and my elbows was to build a pine tanktop shelf unit. It hangs in the unused space above my toilet tank, holding every pomade, soap and lotion I've accumulated in years of smelling nice.

This unit is a great beginner's project with some easy options for making it look professionally handcrafted. To

No.	Ltr.	Item	Dimensions T W L	Material
2	A	Sides	¾ x 6½ x 32	Pine
1	B	Top rail	¾ x 9½ x 18	Pine
1	C	Top shelf	¾ x 5½ x 18	Pine
2	D	Mid & bot shelves	¾ x 5¼ x 18	Pine
1	E	Bottom rail	¾ x 7 x 18	Pine
1	F	Towel bar	⅝ dia. x 18	Dowel

tank heaven **inches**

Other materials: Carpenter's glue, #8 × 1½" wood screws, shellac, paint, stain or urethane. Cornering tools and plug-cutters are available from Lee Valley Tools, 800-871-8158 or www.leevalley.com.

No.	Ltr.	Item	Dimensions T W L	Material
2	A	Sides	19 x 165 x 813	Pine
1	B	Top rail	19 x 242 x 457	Pine
1	C	Top shelf	19 x 140 x 457	Pine
2	D	Mid & bot shelves	19 x 133 x 457	Pine
1	E	Bottom rail	19 x 178 x 457	Pine
1	F	Towel bar	16 dia. x 457	Dowel

tank heaven **millimeters**

Other materials: Carpenter's glue, #8 × 38mm wood screws, shellac, paint, stain or urethane. Cornering tools and plug-cutters are available from Lee Valley Tools, 800-871-8158 or www.leevalley.com.

build it you'll need only a few basic tools, my favorite being the jigsaw.

Tool's Errand

If you're new to woodworking and you're only planning to get one saw, make it a jigsaw. They generate only about as much noise as a sewing machine, plus they perform almost every kind of cut, from straight to swoopy. I recently got the cordless purse model so I'm ready to jig anytime, anywhere.

And while we're talking about tools; whenever you have a birthday or anniversary coming up, ask for clamps. You just can't have too many clamps. You'll need at least one pair of clamps for this project with a minimum span of 20". If you don't have clamps, you're going to have to engage a helper. Clamps are more useful than most helpers, unless the helper brings beer.

And finally, to make your shelves look especially perky, consider buying a plug-cutter bit. This is a cool little device that fits in your drill just like a regular bit. It cuts tiny cylindrical wood plugs that camouflage the screw heads, so the finished project looks tidy.

Cut It Out

Lumber is personality-related, so know yourself. Clear pine is slick and cooperative, but the knotty stuff has more character. Also, if you have a low irritation threshold, avoid boards that are twisted, cupped (the ends of the board are crescent-shaped), split, or sporting "pitch pockets" which are dark spots that ooze sap and defile your work surface, tools and mood.

Take your time in the lumber aisle and use the "eyeballing" technique: Pull a board off the rack and put one end of it on the floor. Then, holding the other end at eye level, scrutinize your subject for twists and warps. Flip it authoritatively, glaring down the length of each surface of the board in turn. If the board is clean and straight, put it on your cart. If it isn't, set it aside and move on to inspecting the next board.

Once you have the boards cut to length, decide on a profile for the side pieces. If you're feeling jaunty and self-assured, mark the shape directly onto the board and cut it out with your jigsaw. If you've gotten into trouble this way in the past, draw the shape on cardboard first and cut it out to be sure it looks okay. Some people like to construct entire mock-ups in cardboard just to test the dimensions. I prefer to wing it and live with my mistakes, which explains my van, but that's another story.

Next draw the wavy shapes for the 18"-long top and bottom rails. To achieve symmetry in your design, take a 9"-wide piece of paper or cardboard and draw a curvy line on it. Cut out the design and trace it onto one half of the 18"-long board. Then flip over the cardboard and trace the design onto the other half of the board. Repeat the process for the bottom border, varying the design a bit so it isn't exactly the same shape as the top.

If you have an earnest reverence for outhouse heritage you may have the

urge to add a crescent moon to your unit. Draw the shape where you want it and drill a generous hole in the middle of the moon. Insert your jigsaw blade into that hole, and proceed to cut out the moon. You should definitely use a scrolling blade for this purpose. A scrolling blade is more delicate than a regular jigsaw blade and can handle tight corners that would make a standard blade buck.

Once you've cut out all your pieces, round over the sharp edges with sandpaper so they're soft and aged-looking. If you find sanding unfulfilling, either lower your expectations or use a cornering tool to ease all the straight edges. Cornering is a hugely satisfying activity, producing lovely curly shavings that can be used later for homemade potpourri.

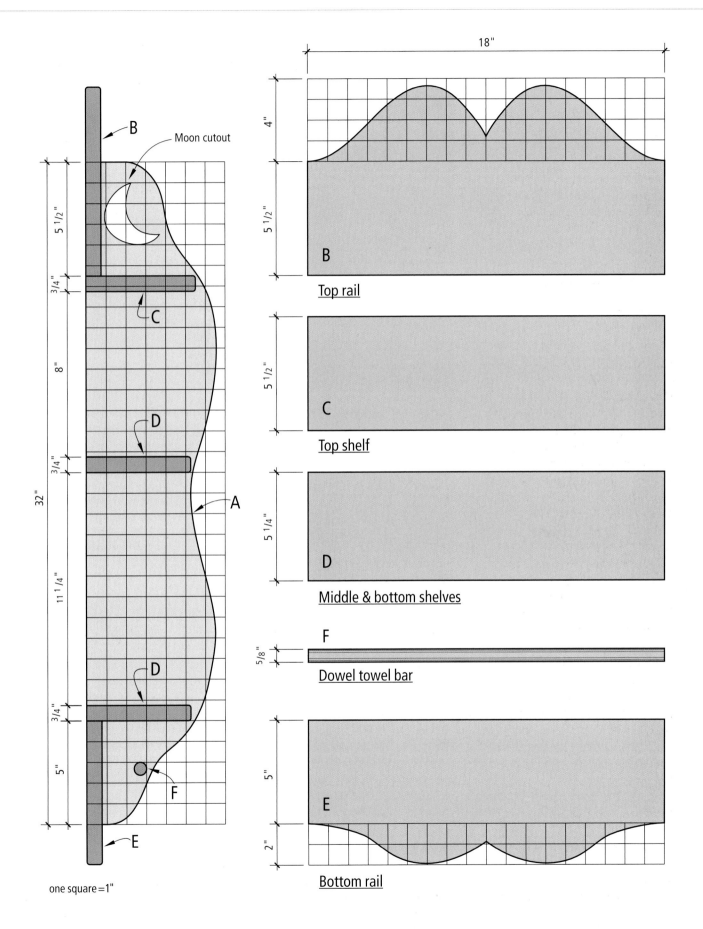

B

Moon cutout

5 1/2"

3/4"

C

8"

D

3/4"

A

32"

11 1/4"

D

3/4"

5"

F

E

one square = 1"

18"

4"

5 1/2"

B

Top rail

5 1/2"

C

Top shelf

5 1/4"

D

Middle & bottom shelves

5/8"

F

Dowel towel bar

5"

E

2"

Bottom rail

Shellac Luster

After all that sanding you're going to want some instant gratification. It's tempting to screw the whole unit together right here, right now. But do yourself a giant favor and put the stain, paint or clear-coat on the individual pieces before you go any further. It is SO MUCH EASIER than having to cover all the multiple surfaces of the shelf unit after it's assembled. Beside that, glue squeeze-out will glom on to bare wood during the assembly process, but if your boards already sport a coat of finish, the glue can be easily wiped off.

My favorite finish is shellac. It's made from the excretions of "lac" bugs that live in trees in India and Indonesia, and if that's not a great conversation starter, I don't know what is. This bug residue is scraped off the trees, then cleaned, filtered and mixed with denatured alcohol to make one of most interesting and least noxious finishes available.

There are two ways to buy shellac: premixed or dry. The premixed shellac has a limited shelf life, so you usually end up having to throw a lot of it out. I prefer to buy dry shellac flakes and mix them with high-quality shellac thinner. Super Blonde shellac from Lee Valley Tools is brilliantly clear, plus it's de-waxed, which means it doesn't water-stain.

Even if you don't work with shellac as your final finish, at least brush a couple of quick dabs of shellac on any knots. This will seal the knots and prevent sap from oozing up under your chosen finish. In fact, shellac is a great primer coat for pretty much any finish except stain, so don't resist using this fine gift from the bug world.

Fit to Be Tried

Now you're ready to dry fit the whole unit. Lay it all out with the sides, shelves and borders in place. This is your opportunity to identify the tallest spray cans in your battery of personal care products. Space the shelves accordingly, so everything fits nicely on the unit when you're done. Clamp

When you're riding your jigsaw around the curves, guide the blade smoothly so you don't create bumps and dings that you'll have to sand out later. Many jigsaws have a dial that allows you to adjust the stroke of the blade to be either gentle or aggressive, depending on the wood you're manipulating and the mood you're in.

A Veritas cornering tool makes short work of softening the edges of pine. It acts as a miniature plane, leaving a smooth radius in its path. If the blade chips or binds, you're working against the grain. Try pulling from the opposite end of the board. Grain lines always get wonky around knots, so you may have to change direction several times, but it's still faster than sanding.

everything together lightly and square the shelves using a speed-square. Now make those clamps nice and tight. Use a pencil to mark a light line on the side pieces under each of the shelves for reference later when you're doing the final assembly under the duress of knowing that the glue is starting to set up.

While all the clamps are in place, predrill pilot holes for your screws so you don't split the shelves when you drive the screws. Then, right on top of the predrilled screw holes, drill larger holes to a depth of $^3/_8$" to make a cavity

for the plugs that will hide the screw heads. To avoid drilling the plug holes too deep, it's a good idea to wrap a piece of masking tape around your drill bit $^3/_8$" from the end so you know when to stop.

Now for the wet fit. Take all the pieces apart and apply a modest bead of glue along the edges of the shelves and borders, plus a dab on each end of the towel bar. Reassemble and clamp everything together, and drive those screws. Use a damp rag to wipe away any oozing glue around the joints.

Shellac has to be applied with a patient, steady hand in smooth, long strokes that don't overlap. Because it's alcohol-based, it dries extremely fast, so there's little downtime. If you're mixing your own shellac, use a good solvent procured from a reliable woodworking supply store.

TIP

As an alternative to cutting your own plugs, you can buy precut hardwood plugs at the hardware store. Hardwood looks funny when used with a softwood like pine; the color of the wood doesn't match, and hardwood isn't as absorbent as pine so the plugs take finish differently and refuse to blend in.

Before inserting each plug into its predrilled hole, place a drop of glue on the bottom of each plug and smear it around a bit.

When you have your unit plugged, wait 20 minutes for the glue to set up. Then use a flush-cut saw to cut each plug flush with the surface of the cabinet. If you don't have a flush-cut saw, you can take the plugs down fairly quickly using a sander loaded with 80-grit sandpaper.

Once the plugs are cut and sanded, touch up the plugs and sides of your unit with shellac or whatever finish you're using.

Just Say 'Yes' to Plugs

Once your screws are in place, fire up the plug-cutter and cut the plugs in a scrap piece of pine.

Once you've cut about 30 plugs, use a knife or screwdriver to pop each plug out of its little hole. They'll pop easier if you lever the knife perpendicular to the grain.

Mount 'Em

Now it's time to mount your unit on the wall. My favorite mounting technique is to screw two 2"-long strips of metal plumber's tape (which has prepunched holes) on the back of the shelf unit, then lift the unit onto waiting nails anchored in studs above the toilet. Finding the studs is a matter of importance, because you don't want your unit crashing down on you while you're otherwise occupied with a good magazine.

Also, it's vital to leave enough room between the toilet tank lid and the shelf unit. If the toilet floods, you need maneuvering room to whip off the lid, plunge your hand into the dank tank and slap the flapper back down. You'll remember this ritual from the first time you knocked something into the toilet, and tried to quietly flush it away.

Plug-cutters come in different sizes and varieties. I used a 1/2" tapered bit to cut my plugs. The resulting plugs are slightly narrower at one end, making them easier to push into the hole later. One safety tip: To prevent the plug-cutter bit from bucking and skating on the wood, set the teeth of the bit in the wood by leaning heavily on your drill before you begin. Keep some weight on the drill as you start the motor.

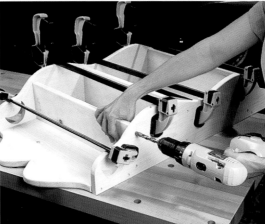

When drilling the countersinks for the plugs, keep your drill as perpendicular to the surface as possible to prevent the plugs from going in at an angle. I went through a troubled phase of having a fish-eye level stuck on the heel of my drill, but it was just distracting.

barrister **bookcases**

Even if you're not a lawyer and don't wear a powdered wig, these bookcases are a smart addition to your home or office.

Not too far from our workshop here in Cincinnati, Globe Furniture made thousands and thousands of these so-called "barrister bookcases" for lawyers and bureaucrats across the nation. Many were made of oak, but the company also made them from other species of wood and even made a steel version.

Though this style of bookcase was first used exclusively by attorneys and government types, the stackable units are now extremely popular (and pricey) in antique stores. And no wonder. You can use them to store just about anything anywhere. While most people use them for books or their favorite collectibles, I know one person who uses them in her bathroom for toiletries.

I designed these bookcases so you can make any number of units that can be stacked on top of one another and side-by-side as well. And there's a com-
plete economy of material use because the top of one also serves as bottom of the case above it. In constructing the three cases shown, I used two different heights for the boxes. The shorter one accommodates books that are 9" tall or less; the larger case accepts books up to 13" tall.

Other than the extra time and expense of more material, it makes a lot of sense to make several boxes because the setups to build these boxes are perfect for the "short production run" approach to building. That means setting up the machine — in this case a router in a table and a drill press — then running the parts. Because it can take longer to accurately set up the machine than to run a part or two, running a few more parts makes real sense. Remember that accuracy is the key to the project because each unit has to be able to mate with the other units.

After you've determined the quantity and size of the cases you want to build, prepare enough wood to glue up the panels you need. Glue up your panels, then sand the joints flush, making sure to keep all the panels the same thickness.

Mill the Cases

The joinery for the cases is straightforward. The plywood back is captured in a rabbet made on the sides and bottom — although the bottom rabbet is stopped ½" from both ends so you can't see it from the outside. Then the bottom is biscuited to the sides. The cases stack on one another using dowels in the tops of each case and holes on the bottom. Begin construction by chucking a straight or rabbeting bit in a router mounted to a table and make the ½" × ½" rabbets in the sides and bottoms.

Now it's time to do some additional routing, to make the groove in the sides for the sliding doors, and some hole drilling. While you can purchase special slides for barrister bookcases, my homemade method is cheaper, works just as well and is almost as easy as installing slides. Each of these steps requires real accuracy, and you must pay attention to which parts are for the right and left sides, fronts and backs, tops and bottoms. The best way to keep this straight is to organize your parts by type, then stack them so they are oriented the way you want them. Marking them with a pencil adds another measure of insurance.

Begin by routing the stopped dadoes in the case sides that make up part of

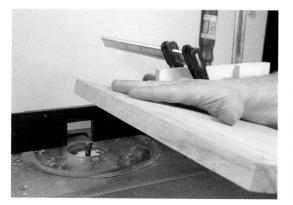

With a ½" straight bit set in a router and mounted in a router table, set the height of the cutter to make a ³⁄₈"-deep cut. Now set up a fence on the router table so the cut starts ⅝" from the edge. Next set a stop on the fence so that the cut you make stops ³⁄₈" from the front edge of the sides. Remember that you will have to change the stop when switching from right to left sides. Because the peg used is ½" thick, you'll need to create a very slight amount of clearance, say ¹⁄₃₂", so the peg moves easily through the dado. Do this by adjusting the fence away from the cutter, then rerun the parts.

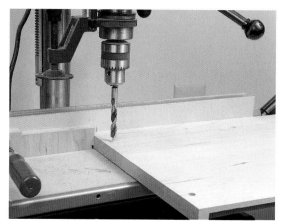

If you want your cases to mate correctly, accuracy is key. Use stop blocks on your drill press when drilling the bottom and use a doweling jig when drilling holes on the sides.

After cutting the slots for the biscuits, assemble the cases. I used polyurethane glue. While not necessary, it does provide a stronger joint because of its ability to provide some glue strength to the end grain/cross-grain joint where the sides join the bottom.

No.	Item	Dimensions T W L	Material
1	Top or bot	¾ x 12⅝ x 34¼	Cherry
2	Sides	¾ x 12 x 13¼*	Cherry
1	Back	½ x 33¼ x 13¾*	Cherry
2	Door rails	¾ x 1¼ x 30⅜	Cherry
2	Door stiles	¾ x 1¼ x 13¹⁄₁₆*	Cherry
1	Base front	1 x 3½ x 34³⁄₁₆	Cherry
2	Base sides	¾ x 3½ x 11⅞	Cherry
1	Base back	¾ x 3 x 32¹¹⁄₁₆	Plywood
1	Glass	⅛ x 12¼ x 30⁵⁄₁₆	
	Glass stops	⅜ x ⁷⁄₁₆ x 8 ft.	Cherry

*Subtract 2" for shorter unit.

No.	Item	Dimensions T W L	Material
1	Top or bot	19 x 321 x 870	Cherry
2	Sides	19 x 305 x 336*	Cherry
1	Back	13 x 844 x 349*	Cherry
2	Door rails	19 x 32 x 772	Cherry
2	Door stiles	19 x 32 x 332*	Cherry
1	Base front	25 x 89 x 869	Cherry
2	Base sides	19 x 89 x 301	Cherry
1	Base back	19 x 76 x 831	Plywood
1	Glass	3 x 311* x 770	
	Glass stops	10 x 11 x 2438	Cherry

*Subtract 51mm for shorter unit.

barrister bookcases **inches**

barrister bookcases **millimeters**

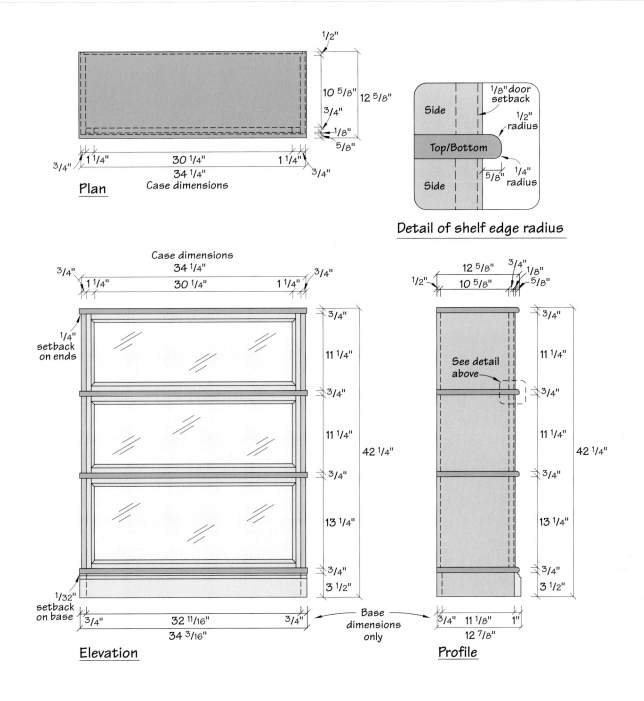

1/2"

10 5/8" 12 5/8"

3/4"

1/8"

5/8"

3/4" 1 1/4" 30 1/4" 1 1/4" 3/4"

34 1/4"

Plan Case dimensions

1/8" door setback

1/2" radius

Side

Top/Bottom

Side

1/4" radius

5/8"

Detail of shelf edge radius

Case dimensions

34 1/4"

3/4" 1 1/4" 30 1/4" 1 1/4" 3/4"

1/4" setback on ends

3/4"

11 1/4"

3/4"

11 1/4"

3/4"

42 1/4"

13 1/4"

3/4"

3 1/2"

1/32" setback on base

3/4" 32 11/16" 3/4"

34 3/16"

Elevation

Base dimensions only

12 5/8" 3/4" 1/8"

1/2" 10 5/8" 5/8"

3/4"

11 1/4"

See detail above

3/4"

11 1/4"

3/4"

42 1/4"

13 1/4"

3/4"

3 1/2"

3/4" 11 1/8" 1"

12 7/8"

Profile

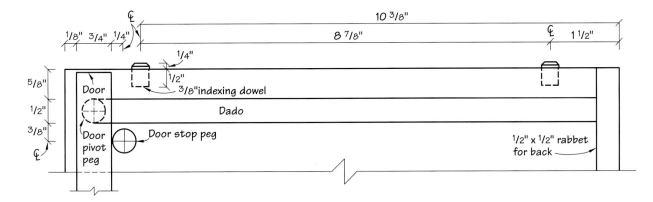

10 3/8"

1/8" 3/4" 1/4" 8 7/8" 1 1/2"

1/4"

1/2"

3/8" indexing dowel

5/8" Door

Dado

1/2"

3/8" Door pivot peg Door stop peg

1/2" x 1/2" rabbet for back

the sliding door mechanism. The other part of the mechanism is simply a peg inserted into the edge of the door.

Make Perfect Holes

Now drill the holes in the case bottoms. These holes are used to receive the indexing pins that are inserted in the top edges of the sides. This interlocking quality keeps the cases from sliding while stacked atop one another and holds the sides in position. Remember that the holes are drilled in the bottom piece and line up with each case's sides. Set up the drill press with a ⅜"- diameter bit, using the fence and a stop block, and drill the holes as indicated in the diagrams to a depth of ⅜". Bear in mind that the holes are a different distance from the front and back edge so the fence setup must change accordingly.

Now drill the corresponding holes in the top edges of the sides, again to a depth of ⅜". These holes are for the dowel pins. Accuracy is key: I used a self-centering doweling jig for drilling these holes. Mark the drilling locations carefully. Refer to the diagram on page 25 for drilling locations.

Biscuit the Sides

Next cut the biscuit slots for joining the sides to the bottom. I used three biscuits in each side: a #20 size in the middle and back, and a #10 in the front. I used the #10 so the slot wouldn't interfere with the hole drilled in the bottom. The last thing to do before final assembly is to run a roundover detail on the front edge of the bottoms. To make my profile, I used a ½" radius bit on the top edge and a ¼" radius bit on the bottom edge. Again, use the router table and fence for the cut, even if you have router bits with guide bearings on them. You can rely on the bearing for the first cut, but on the second cut the bearing would ride on the previously cut radius which sweeps away from the edge.

Assemble and glue the sides to the bottoms. I set the case backs in place to help keep the assembly square during the glue up. Here's how I glued these up: Put glue on the mating parts and set them in place. Then set in the back and clamp across the back and sides. Next, while making sure the back edge of the side is flush to the back edge of the bottom, clamp the side and

bottom from top to bottom. With all the clamps in place, check for square and adjust as needed. Do not attach the backs until after finishing.

Next I made the base of the bookcases. Rout the ogee profile on the top edge of the front piece only, before biscuiting and gluing the base together. The sides simply abut the back side of the front piece, and the plywood back piece abuts into the sides. The back piece is narrower than the sides and front so leave some space at the floor for any base moulding on your floors. Attach the back piece flush to the top of the base assembly. I also elected not to attach the base permanently to one of the cases. Instead I screwed indexing blocks to the case bottom that allow the lower case to nest into the base. This allows you to level the base when you install it and simply stack the cases on top.

Frame and Panel Doors

The frames for the glass doors are the last chore to tackle before moving on to sanding and finishing. Because I wanted the relatively small doors to have a delicate appearance, I made my stiles

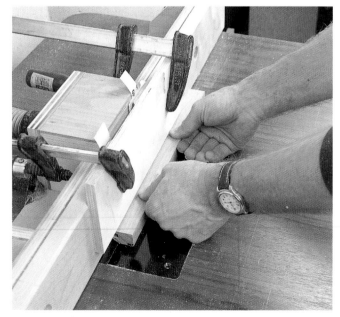

First run the ogee detail on the inside edges of both the stiles and rails. Set the height of the cutter so it leaves just a slight bead on the face of the parts, say ¹/₃₂". After running the parts, switch to the coping cutter and cut the matching, opposite detail on the ends of the rails only. Make sure you use a back-up block, also called a coping block, to stabilize the narrow part while running it across the router bit.

A simple block made to index off the top edge of the side, along with a dowel center, marks the drilling center for the dowel pivot guide. Use the dowel center's point to insert a ¹/₂" brad point drill point and make the hole.

and rails just $1\frac{1}{4}$" wide. For a strong corner joint and a pretty detail on the inside edge of the frame, I used a matched stile-and-rail router bit set normally used for frame-and-panel doors. The nice ogee detail I used echos the detail on the base, and complements the rounded front edge of the case bottoms.

Again, make sure you cut your stiles and rails to the exact length needed using a stop block. This will help ensure that your frame is square. Because the router bits are intended to be used with fixed panels, and the glass needs to be removable, it's necessary to cut away part of the edge detail on the back, changing it from a groove to a rabbet. Using a table saw makes it a simple procedure for the rails because you can run the part all the way through. For the stiles, however, you need to make a stopped cut because the piece you leave at the ends is part of the "mortise" joint made by the matching router profiles. Mark the stiles from the ends where you want to stop the cut (it can vary slightly depending on the cutters you use), then mark the table saw's fence at the point where the blade projects above the table when it is set to the correct height for the cut you're making. While holding the part firmly to the fence, slowly lower it onto the blade with the motor running, then cut the part to the matching lines on both the part and the saw fence.

Now you can glue up the stile and rail assembly, making sure you check for square and adjust as needed. When dry, chisel out the corner of the back of the stile where the waste piece remained from the stop cut you just made.

Critical Dowel Location

Check the fit of the doors. You should have a $\frac{1}{16}$" gap on the sides and bottom and a $\frac{1}{8}$" gap left for the top. This allows the door to pivot up without touching the piece above it. If the fit is good, drill a $\frac{1}{2}$" hole in the door's edge that's $\frac{1}{2}$" deep. Locate the hole in the center of the edge so the hole centers $\frac{13}{16}$" down from the top edge. Use your combination square as a marking gauge and a doweling jig for accurate drilling. Drill these holes on both edges of each door. Insert a $\frac{7}{8}$" length of dowel or other $\frac{1}{2}$" rod into the door edge. Place the doors in the side grooves of the case, which is easily done with the top open. Bring the doors forward and gently lower them down into position.

Glass Installation and Finishing

The last bit of fussing with the doors consists of setting the pin below the groove where the doors slide. Carefully positioning the pin provides not only the resting spot for the doors when open, but also coaxes them into the proper location at the top when closed. Lastly, cut and fit the $\frac{3}{8}$" × $\frac{7}{16}$" strips that will hold the glass in place on the back side of the frames.

Sand your parts with 120- and 150-grit paper using a random-orbit sander. Also make sure no glue was left behind that would splotch a nice finish. For the final finish I tried something I'd never done before. I added a slight amount of oil-base stain to boiled linseed oil. Linseed oil on cherry brings out the grain of the wood more than a film finish like varnish, shellac or lacquer does. The wee bit of color added (I used about a thimbleful of stain to 10 ounces of oil) gave the new cherry a bit of maturity. I tend to think that new cherry without any color added looks anemic, but too much color causes cherry to blotch if applied full strength.

If you choose to use an oil-only finish, apply a couple more coats of boiled linseed oil, making sure you thoroughly wipe off all excess oil after applying. For my bookcases, I allowed the oil to dry overnight then sprayed the pieces with clear lacquer. Brushing on varnish, shellac or polyurethane will work as well. Finally, put your doors back into the cases and screw the backs into the sides and bottom.

When it comes time to set up your barrister bookcases, the modular construction and variety of arrangements should prove a real asset. That is, unless you can't agree with your "significant other" about how they should be arranged. In that case, you might just need a barrister to settle the bookcase dispute.

To install the glass, use wood stops with mitered corners cut to fit in the rabbets. An easy way to hold the stops in place is by using $\frac{1}{8}$" fender washers and screws. Simply screw them into the frame with part of the washer lapping over the stop. I clipped the ones on the door sides so they wouldn't hit the dowel on which the door rests when it slides back into the cabinet.

built-in **bookcases**

Learn the secret of the 'fitting strip'
and you can make anything built-in.

In almost every American home there's the odd corner where not a single piece of furniture looks right. You know what I'm talking about: the weird space beside the fireplace, the interior corner in the solarium, the space next to the sliding glass door. You've probably thought to yourself that a custom built-in cabinet would do the trick. In my home, that space was next to the fireplace. Here's how I turned that liability into an attractive asset that adds value to my home.

Rabbets & Dadoes

Face frame cabinets are one of the easiest types of cabinets to build. Start by cutting the carcass sides and bottom. To support the bottom, cut a $^3/_8$"-deep × $^3/_4$"-wide dado on the inside of each side so the top of the dado is 3" up from the bottom. Next, cut a $^1/_2$"-deep × $^3/_4$" rabbet on the inside top edge of each side to accept the support rails.

The first step in making this cabinet

built-in rather than free-standing is routing a rabbet on one of the sides. If your wall is perfect and square, you're in great shape and won't have to do any fitting.

In my corner cabinet, the interior side was ripped a second time to 20$^1/_2$". This allows the back to simply overlay the entire back edge of the interior side without the worry of a rabbet. If the cabinet were being mounted to a wall where both sides would be visible, both sides would be made with a rabbeted back edge.

Assemble the lower cabinet using glue and clamps, strategically placed nails, or for extra strength and less nails, cleats can be used to attach the sides to the bottom from underneath. Square up the cabinet and temporarily attach the back to support the cabinet.

The upper shelving section is built

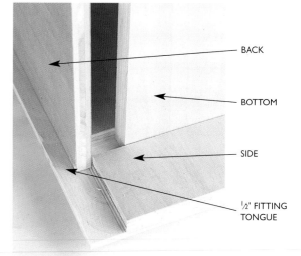

BACK

BOTTOM

SIDE

$^1/_2$" FITTING TONGUE

For my corner cabinet, the visible side has a $^1/_2$"-thick × 1" rabbet cut the length of the back edge. This allows room for the $^1/_2$" back to fit in the rabbet and another $^1/_2$" tongue, which is fit to the wall with a jigsaw or hand plane.

No.	Item	Dimensions T W L	Material
	built-in bookcases **inches**		
LOWER BOOKSHELVES			
2	Sides	³/₄ x 21¹/₂ x 30¹/₄	Cherry plywood
1	Bottom	³/₄ x 20¹/₂ x 29¹/₂	Cherry plywood
2	Support rails	³/₄ x 3 x 29³/₄	Cherry plywood
1	Back	¹/₂ x 30 x 27¹/₄	Cherry plywood
2	Fitting strips	¹/₂ x 1¹/₂ x 30¹/₄	Cherry
2	Facing stiles	³/₄ x 1¹/₂ x 30¹/₄	Cherry
2	Facing rails	³/₄ x 3 x 27¹/₄	Cherry
4	Door stiles	³/₄ x 1¹/₂ x 24¹/₄	Cherry
4	Door rails	³/₄ x 1¹/₂ x 13⁵/₈	Cherry
2	Door panels	¹/₄ x 11⁵/₈ x 22¹/₄	Cherry plywood
1	Top	³/₄ x 22¹/₄ x 31³/₄	Cherry plywood
1	Top edging	³/₄ x 1¹/₂ x 32¹/₂	Cherry
1	Top edging	³/₄ x 1¹/₂ x 23	Cherry
UPPER BOOKSHELVES			
2	Sides	³/₄ x 9 x 54	Cherry plywood
1	Top	³/₄ x 9 x 29¹/₂	Cherry plywood
3	Shelves	³/₄ x 7³/₄ x 28³/₄	Cherry plywood
3	Shelf facings	³/₄ x 1¹/₂ x 28³/₄	Cherry
2	Facing stiles	³/₄ x 1¹/₂ x 54	Cherry
1	Facing rail	³/₄ x 3 x 27¹/₄	Cherry
1	Back	¹/₂ x 30 x 53¹/₄	Cherry plywood
2	Fitting strips	¹/₂ x 1¹/₂ x 54	Cherry
1	Support rail	³/₄ x 2¹/₂ x 28³/₄	Cherry

No.	Item	Dimensions T W L	Material
	built-in bookcases **millimeters**		
LOWER BOOKSHELVES			
2	Sides	19 x 546 x 768	Cherry plywood
1	Bottom	19 x 521 x 750	Cherry plywood
2	Support rails	19 x 76 x 756	Cherry plywood
1	Back	13 x 762 x 692	Cherry plywood
2	Fitting strips	13 x 38 x 768	Cherry
2	Facing stiles	19 x 38 x 768	Cherry
2	Facing rails	19 x 76 x 692	Cherry
4	Door stiles	19 x 38 x 616	Cherry
4	Door rails	19 x 38 x 346	Cherry
2	Door panels	6 x 295 x 565	Cherry plywood
1	Top	19 x 565 x 806	Cherry plywood
1	Top edging	19 x 38 x 826	Cherry
1	Top edging	19 x 38 x 584	Cherry
UPPER BOOKSHELVES			
2	Sides	19 x 229 x 1372	Cherry plywood
1	Top	19 x 229 x 750	Cherry plywood
3	Shelves	19 x 197 x 730	Cherry plywood
3	Shelf facings	19 x 38 x 730	Cherry
2	Facing stiles	19 x 38 x 1372	Cherry
1	Facing rail	19 x 76 x 692	Cherry
1	Back	13 x 762 x 1352	Cherry plywood
2	Fitting strips	13 x 38 x 1372	Cherry
1	Support rail	19 x 64 x 730	Cherry

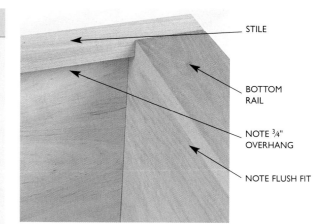

STILE

BOTTOM RAIL

NOTE ³/₄" OVERHANG

NOTE FLUSH FIT

Mill the facing rails and stiles to size, then glue the frames together with biscuits, remembering to check for square. When the glue has dried, sand the inside frame surface flush, then glue and clamp the frames to the front of the cabinet carcasses.

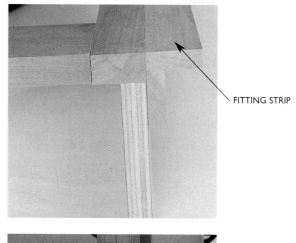

FITTING STRIP

FITTING STRIP

Both pieces of the fitting strip are made of solid ¹/₂" cherry. For the inset doors the fitting strip is flush. For overlay doors, attach the strip forward to match the overlay (above).

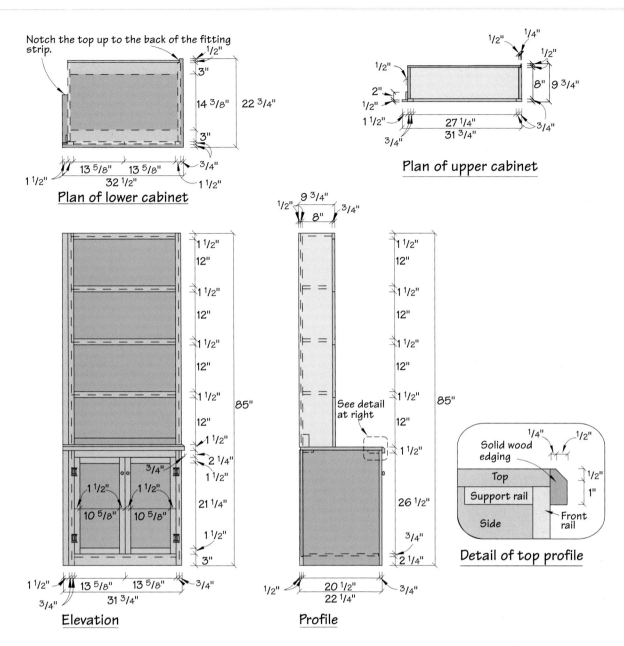

Notch the top up to the back of the fitting strip.

Plan of lower cabinet

Plan of upper cabinet

Elevation

Profile

Solid wood edging

Top

Support rail

Side

Front rail

Detail of top profile

in the same manner, but with the dado cut at the top of the sides, 1½" down from the top. The lower support rail at the bottom of the unit is biscuited between the sides, so run the same rabbet on the back edges of each side and temporarily attach the back for extra support.

Face Frames

Make the two face frames. The stiles of the lower cabinet overhang the inside of the cabinet by ¾", but the bottom rail overhangs the bottom only a fraction of an inch on the inside. The outside overhang should be sanded flush to the cabinet after gluing.

The top for the lower cabinet is simply cut to size from plywood, then a solid cherry edge is glued and biscuited to the two visible edges with a miter joint at the corner. I ran a ½" chamfer on the top edge to soften the edge of the top.

Fitting Strips

The most important piece of the built-in part of the cabinetry is next. Referred to as fitting strips, these are simply L-shaped strips that are screwed to the wall side of the cabinet during installation.

The shelves are the next step in construction. Cut the shelves to size

and biscuit and glue a ¾" × 1½" solid cherry rail to the front edge. This is called a "dropped edge" and not only gives the shelves a more substantial appearance, it keeps the shelves from bowing under the weight of books. The shelves are held in place with adjustable shelf pins which can be located and drilled to suit your needs.

Half-Lap Doors

The butterfly hinges I used don't require any mortising, but you do need to be careful to align the doors correctly when attaching the hinges.

The interior of the lower cabinet can be adjusted to suit your needs. On the piece shown, I installed three interior drawers compartmentalized for video-tape storage.

I finished the piece using a cherry oil-based stain and two coats of satin finish lacquer, giving the piece a rich appearance.

Installation

At this point you might want to take a couple of minutes to consider how the cabinets will be used. If you're adding any lighting or stereo components to the cabinets, consider your wiring options. Also consider ventilation for the stereo.

Start the installation by preparing the space where the cabinet will go. If the room is carpeted, the cabinet can sit right on top of the carpeting. This cabinet has been designed to work without a base moulding. If you have grooved hardwood floors, the cabinet base against the floor will show off these grooves. If this offends you, a small quarter-round moulding can be added after installation. Any existing baseboard in the cabinet's location can be marked and cut in place with a backed saw so the cabinet will slip into place (from above if it's a corner cabinet). Or the baseboard can be removed, cut and reattached after the cabinet is installed. A third option is to cope the back of the cabinet and the fitting strip to match the base moulding and allow the cabinet to cover the baseboard.

With the space prepared, put the cabinet in place, allowing space for the fitting strip (or with the fitting strip attached), square it up and level it up front-to-back and side-to-side using shims. Then check the fit against the walls. If you're lucky you won't have to touch a thing, but more likely than not you'll need to use the scribing method shown at right. The face frame could have been designed to extend beyond the cabinet and serve as a fitting strip, but the removable fitting strip is a lot easier to remove, mill and replace than the whole cabinet.

Put the cabinet back in place and again check the fit. If everything looks

good, the cabinet can be screwed in place against the wall. Locate the studs behind the cabinet. Hopefully you can catch two. If not, a molly in the wall can provide a second attachment location. Mark the stud locations on the cabinet back and drill a clearance hole, then screw the cabinet in place. Make sure you use a long enough screw, 3" is preferable. Don't overtighten the screw, it needs only to pull the cabinet to the wall, not correct any bow in the drywall, that's what the scribing is for.

Before putting the top in place, drill two clearance holes in each of the support rails to attach the top after fitting. Next put the top in place and check its fit against the wall. Then plane or cut to provide the best joint. Place the upper bookcase unit on the top, and again fit, scribe and plane or cut the back edge and fitting strip to match. With the bookcase fit to the walls, lightly mark the side location on the top, then remove the bookcase. Drill holes through the top — two per side — then remove the top from the lower cabinet and attach the upper case to the top with screws.

The upper assembly should fit into place with a few inches of clearance on top. Screw the top to the lower cabinet through the support strips. A couple screws through the upper case's back at the very top will secure it to the wall. Hang the doors, put the shelves in place and you're ready to fill the cabinets.

The doors are a simple but classic flat panel construction using half-lap joinery at the corners. The $1/4$" cherry plywood panels are captured in a $1/2$" groove run in the stiles and rails prior to assembly. Since they are inset doors, check the sizes in the Materials List against your actual opening. The doors should be a hair oversized to allow for fitting.

Take a compass, and with the legs separated to the width of the widest gap between wall and cabinet, scribe a line down the back edge and against the front of the fitting strip. Remove the cabinet and cut almost to the scribe line with a coping saw or jigsaw. Then clean the cut with a plane.

boating
bookshelf

Build this rustic book-
shelf with basic tools,
and without cutting your
old canoe in half.

On a Sunday outing I wan-
dered into a small town
and came upon a hand-
made sign along the side
of the road that simply
said "FISH DECOYS, OPEN." What a
discovery, I wasn't aware there were decoys used to attract fish. It so happened
that this modest little shop behind the
owner's home was the studio of S. Rob-
bins, one of the most highly regarded
carvers and painters of fish decoys. As
he worked at his bench, I browsed
through the shop showroom and ad-
mired his beautifully detailed work.

In one corner were examples of
what I thought was his most interesting
work. They were displayed on shelves
that had been fitted into an ancient
canoe that had been cut in half at its
midsection and stood on end. Not having a canoe to lop in half, I came up
with this shelving project as a variation
on his theme.

Even after a fair amount of designing, I'll say that the hull geometry un-

No.	Item	Dimensions T W L	Material
		boating bookshelf **inches**	
1	Bottom	$^3/_8$ x 24 x 72	Bead board ply
1	Bottom shelf	$^3/_4$ x 12 x 18	Birch ply
1	A Shelf	$^3/_4$ x 12 x 22	Birch ply
1	B Shelf	$^3/_4$ x 12 x 24	Birch ply
1	C Shelf	$^3/_4$ x 12 x 24	Birch ply
1	D Shelf	$^3/_4$ x 12 x 20$^1/_2$	Birch ply
1	Fwrd blkhd	$^3/_4$ x 12 x 12	Birch ply
1	Stem	$1^1/_2$ x $3^1/_2$ x 12	2×4 stock
1	Stem cap	$^3/_4$ x 14 x 10	Birch ply (shape to fit)
2	Top rails	$^3/_4$ x $1^1/_8$ x 72	Pine (cut to fit)
1	Stern rail	$^3/_4$ x $1^1/_2$ x $16^3/_4$	Pine
1	Stem cover	$^1/_2$ x 1 x $12^3/_8$	Pine
1	Stem cover	$^1/_2$ x $1^3/_8$ x $12^3/_8$	Pine
16	Siding	$^1/_8$ x $1^7/_8$ x 78	Temp hrdbrd (Duron)

Start at the stern. Place the stick to the inside of the nail, then bend it around the outside of the nails at the other shelf locations, then inside the nail at the bow. Draw a pencil line following the stick. Repeat the process for the other side.

No.	Item	Dimensions T W L	Material
		boating bookshelf **millimeters**	
1	Bottom	10 x 610 x 1829	Bead board ply
1	Bottom shelf	19 x 305 x 457	Birch ply
1	A Shelf	19 x 305 x 559	Birch ply
1	B Shelf	19 x 305 x 610	Birch ply
1	C Shelf	19 x 305 x 610	Birch ply
1	D Shelf	19 x 305 x 521	Birch ply
1	Fwrd blkhd	19 x 305 x 305	Birch ply
1	Stem	38 x 89 x 305	2×4 stock
1	Stem cap	19 x 356 x 254	Birch ply (shape to fit)
2	Top rails	19 x 29 x 1829	Pine (cut to fit)
1	Stern rail	19 x 38 x 425	Pine
1	Stem cover	13 x 25 x 315	Pine
1	Stem cover	13 x 35 x 315	Pine
16	Siding	3 x 47 x 1981	Temp hrdbrd (Duron)

BOW

Here you can see that the shelves fit inside the layout of the "hull" on the plywood. Note that I was still planning to use a curved bow at this stage. I soon gave this up and opted for straight-sided shelves.

derwent a "midstream" change from how I had originally envisioned it. You see, I wanted the sides of the boat to curve not only bow to stern, but also top to bottom. You'll notice that the ribs, or shelves, of the hull curve on the outside. I discovered, when trying to apply the "siding" to the ribs, that the compound curves created by the curve in the ribs caused the siding to head in odd directions.

After scratching my head and reading about lapstrake boat building, I decided I could live with a hull that was straight from top to bottom. The rest was smooth sailing.

A Word About Materials

During a trip to the lumberyard I also learned that my initial plan to use

clapboard siding to cover the hull was too expensive. My alternative was $^1/_8$"-thick tempered hardboard called Duron. It's great for this application because the material is dense so the sawed edges don't fuzz up. The yard also had $^3/_8$"-thick plywood that sported a bead board detail that looked appropriately "boaty," so I bought it for the vessel's bottom.

Lay Out Your Bottom

Before cutting any other material, first make a full-size layout of the boat bottom showing the outside shape and the location of the shelves. Start by cutting the bead board plywood oversize to 26" × 74". Strike a center line on the back side of the plywood from its top to bottom.

Next lay out the shelf locations. Use the diagram on page 35 to establish the curve of the boat side.

To establish the proper bends, rip a piece of bendable wood to $^1/_4$" thick and about 84" long: I used $^3/_4$" clear pine. Pound a small finish nail at the location of each shelf in your plywood. Place the nail on the edge of the shelf line at the bottom shelf, then place the next nails at each shelf edge, less the $^1/_4$" thickness of the bending stick. Do this at all shelf end locations, and set the last nail at the bow on the center line. Then insert your bending stick into the nails.

Cut Out the Shelves

Next, verify the shelf lengths on your layout against the lengths given in the

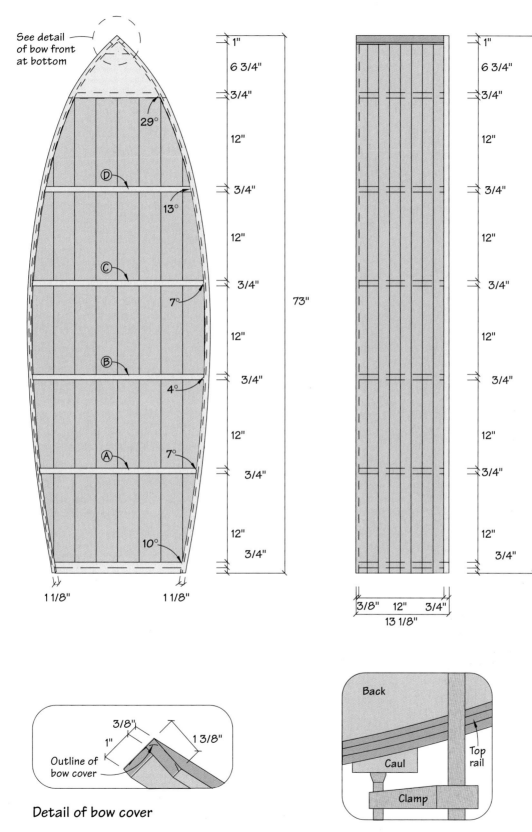

See detail
of bow front
at bottom

29°

Ⓓ
13°

Ⓒ
7°

Ⓑ
4°

Ⓐ
7°

10°

1"
6 3/4"
3/4"
12"
3/4"
12"
3/4"
12"
3/4"
12"
3/4"
12"
3/4"

73"

1 1/8"   1 1/8"

1"
6 3/4"
3/4"
12"
3/4"
12"
3/4"
12"
3/4"
12"
3/4"
12"
3/4"

73"

3/8"   12"   3/4"
13 1/8"

3/8"
1"
1 3/8"

Outline of
bow cover

Detail of bow cover

Back

Caul

Top
rail

Clamp

Detail of clamping caul

I used an L-shaped piece of plywood to keep my shelves square to the bottom as I fastened them. Clamp it to the shelf and back as shown, then screw the shelves in place.

I made this simple jig to safely and accurately cut the bevel on the hardboard siding. Sandwich a scrap piece of hardboard between the two plywood pieces to create the opening through which you push the long strips of siding. Set your table saw to cut a 7° angle and run the hardboard through the slot.

Materials List. Use the degree settings given in the diagram on page 35 for cutting your shelf ends. These angles will give you a better surface to nail and glue to when applying the siding for the hull.

With the shelves complete, cut out the stem piece from a short length of 2×4. The actual point of the stem piece turned out to be a 45° angle.

Now cut out the bottom following your drawing. You're cutting from the back side of the plywood using a jigsaw so there won't be any tear-out on the good side.

Begin Assembly
Before attaching the shelves, apply veneer tape to the shelves' front edges. This will cover the plywood edge, giving it the appearance of solid wood. Veneer edging is available preglued and is easy to apply using an ordinary iron. Trim any veneer overhang and presand the shelves. Next, drill and countersink holes through the boat bottom and screw the shelves in place.

Cut the Skin
To prepare the ⅛" hardboard siding, first rip 16 pieces to 1⅞" wide. To make this task easier, I first ripped two 9" widths off the big 4' × 8' sheet. I then crosscut the pieces to about 78" in length, leaving enough to cover the side and trim to length when done. The last step in preparing the pieces is saw-

ing a bevel on one edge to allow over-lapping pieces to seat together without producing a gap.

Attach the Siding
To apply the siding, set your craft upside down on a level surface so you can nail the first piece starting at the bottom. Because the hardboard is too dense to nail through without splitting, first drill clearance holes. I didn't use a lot of nails, just enough to keep the strips in place, but I did use a modest dab of Liquid Nails at the fastening point for each strip. Start nailing at the bow with the strip length overhanging slightly.

When one side is completely covered, trim any overhang at the bow so it doesn't interfere with attaching the siding on the next side. It need not be

a pretty cut because the bow will eventually be capped. For now leave any excess at the stern. Proceed with covering the second side. When done, let your project sit for a couple hours and allow the adhesive to cure.

Before trimming the siding at the stern, use some scrap to make a ¾" buildup and apply it with glue and nails to the front and side edges of the bottom shelf. With the buildups in place, use the edge to guide your saw to trim the overhang.

Laminating the Top Rails
Because you can't bend a piece wide enough to cover the top edge of the boat's sides, it's necessary to laminate the wood into the required shape. This is done by cutting thinner, bendable strips, then gluing them back to-

After the first piece is in place, use a 1⅝"-wide spacer block to mark a pencil line at each shelf location to give you the location of the next piece of siding. Apply adhesive to the edge of each shelf where the strip will be nailed. Use only one nail at each shelf and two nails at the stern and stem. Locate the nails so they are covered by the next strip.

gether on a form using clamps. While this can be a lot of trouble, we're in luck because the necessary bending form is already made — it's the bottom of the boat!

Start by cutting ¾"-thick pine into ⅜"- wide strips that are about 72" long. Cut six strips in all. Before gluing up, have three clamps ready and make two clamping cauls each for the stern and bow end. The caul's face that contacts the wood strips should closely match the contour of the boat's shape, while the edge that goes against the clamp should be square to the clamp face. These cauls are easy to make and need not be perfect. Make two cauls for the bow end that match the bulkhead, and another two cauls that match the side shape at the stern.

After both strips have dried, clean them up with sandpaper, then cut them to length. So that the top rails properly butt the stem cap at the bow, cut the rails at an angle and place them so they overlap the front edge of the forward bulkhead by ½". This will give you enough surface to nail the stem cap to the bulkhead.

Make the stem cap by setting a slightly oversize piece of plywood in position on the bow. Mark the bow shape on the underside of the plywood with a pencil. Then measure the overhang of the top rail on the outside of the boat and add that dimension, approximately ⅝", to the pencil lines to deter-

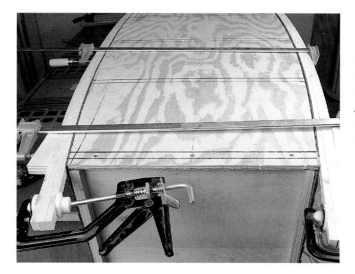

You'll be better off with an extra set of hands when you begin gluing up the strips, so hail a mate for some help. If you're on your own just glue one set of strips at a time and you'll be okay.

mine the necessary overhang of the stem cap. Use your jigsaw to cut the shape, then use the edge tape veneer to cover the plywood edge. When done, nail and glue the stem cap in place.

Stem Cover and Stern Rail

Only two more pieces, and the hard work will be done. Fashion the stem cover following the diagram on page 35. I shaped the outside to a rough

form using a block plane. When done, nail it in place. The stern rail bridges the two side rails at the bottom. Match the angles at the ends formed by the rails, and nail in place.

Before sanding and finishing, set the nails and fill with putty. Sand only the wood parts and the Duron where you have used putty. I finished the wood parts with one coat of polyurethane to protect it from my green paint, then painted the hull with two coats. Lastly, I lightly sanded the first coat of polyurethane and brushed on a final coat.

Now, if I only had some of those fabulous looking fish decoys to display in my Boating Bookshelf.

Stem cover

Outline of top rail

Outline of boat siding

Stem

Full-size diagram of stem and bow bulkhead

shaker
hanging shelf

Show off your china or glassware
with this easy-to-build project.

shaker hanging shelf **inches**

No.	Item	Dimensions T W L	Material
2	Ends	$^1/2$ x $6^1/2$ x 24	Poplar
1	Shelf	$^1/2$ x $4^1/4$ x $29^1/2$	Poplar
1	Shelf	$^1/2$ x $5^1/4$ x $29^1/2$	Poplar
1	Shelf	$^1/2$ x $6^1/2$ x $29^1/2$	Poplar
3	Cross braces	$^1/2$ x $1^1/2$ x 30	Poplar

shaker hanging shelf **millimeters**

No.	Item	Dimensions T W L	Material
2	Ends	13 x 165 x 610	Poplar
1	Shelf	13 x 108 x 750	Poplar
1	Shelf	13 x 133 x 750	Poplar
1	Shelf	13 x 165 x 750	Poplar
3	Cross braces	13 x 38 x 762	Poplar

First prepare your stock according to the sizes given in the Materials List. Then lay out and cut the $^1/2$" × $^1/4$"-deep dadoes in the end pieces. Also make the $^1/2$" × $1^1/2$" notches in the ends to receive the cross braces below each shelf.

Lay out one end piece, cut the 8° angle on the front, then sand the edges. Use this end as a template for cutting the other end. Then clamp the two pieces together and sand both front edges so they match perfectly.

The dimensions given for the shelves are a little oversize in width to allow for fitting. Cut them, then make an 8° saw cut on the front edge of the shelves to match the angle of the end. Reset the saw blade to square, and cut the shelves to finished width. Sand all of the parts when this is done. Now set up a router with a $^1/4$" round-nose bit. Rout the plate grooves on the shelves at the locations given in the diagram.

Using 6d nails and a $^1/16$" pilot bit, nail the shelves and cross braces into the ends. Apply wood glue to the inside of the dadoes and notches, as well as the top edge of the cross brace support. Then clamp the cross brace to the shelf until the glue dries. For a more traditional look, take an old nail set and grind the tip to a slightly rectangular point. When you set the nails, there will be the impression that cut nails were used for assembly.

Finally, putty the holes and touch-up sand. Finish with a dark cherry gel stain along with three coats of a clear top coat such as varnish, shellac, lacquer or oil. If you hang a Shaker peg rail on the wall and use 10" or 15" centers for the peg locations, the shelf will hang nicely. Use equal length pieces of rawhide tied through the holes near the top of the ends to hang the shelf on the pegs.

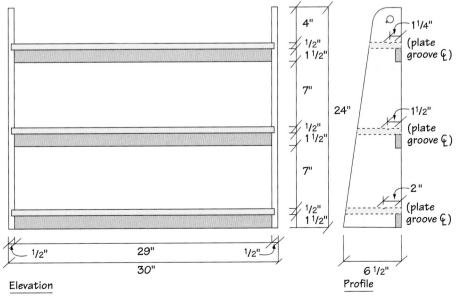

4"

1/2"

1 1/2"

7"

1/2"

1 1/2"

7"

1/2"

1 1/2"

24"

1 1/4"

(plate groove ℄)

1 1/2"

(plate groove ℄)

2"

(plate groove ℄)

1/2"   29"   1/2"

30"

Elevation

6 1/2"

Profile

country **dry sink**

Though this dry sink won't store
pitchers of milk fresh from the cow,
it will give your kitchen an old-time
feel that no modern cabinet could.

Traditional American dry sinks were made from yellow pine and had deep wooden troughs on top that were useful for storing pitchers, churns and buckets of liquids. Now that we've got refrigerators and ice makers, the dry sink has graduated to become an expensive item at antique markets.

This updated version preserves the form of the traditional dry sink, with its high splash guard on back and storage down below, but I've altered a few key components. Instead of a sunken wooden trough on top, I've added two drawers. And instead of yellow pine, this dry sink is made from curly maple. Put the finished project in your kitchen to add a country touch to a farm home, or use it as a buffet in an informal dining room.

Traditional Construction

I build all my casework the same way, and I'm convinced that these methods

will ensure that the furniture will be around for a long time. Begin by building the face frame of the cabinet because most of the cabinet dimensions are based on the face frame. I use mortise-and-tenon joinery to join the rails and stiles. I make the tenons on all the rails 1" long, and all the mortises $1\frac{1}{16}$" deep, which will ensure your tenons won't bottom out in your mortises and give some space for excess glue to go. Dry fit the face frame parts, then put glue in the mortises and glue up all the rails and stiles. Start with the center rail and stile, and work out.

Doors Next

Once the glue is dry from the face frame, I like to make my doors. They are easier to hang and fit while the face frame can be laid flat on my bench. The doors are built much the same way as the face frame, with 1"-long tenons on the rails. To hold the panel in place, I plow a $\frac{3}{8}$" × $\frac{3}{8}$" groove down the inside edge of all the door parts. Be sure to make the tenons on the rails haunched because of this groove.

Once you have the rails and stiles fit, measure the opening for the panel and cut your stock to size, making sure that you leave a $\frac{1}{8}$" gap all around to accommodate wood movement in the panel. I cut an 8° bevel on the edges of the panel using my shaper, though you can easily cut this bevel by tilting the blade about 12° on your table saw. Finish sand the panel and add one coat of stain.

Place the panel in the groove, glue up the mortise-and-tenon joints and clamp the doors. You'll notice that I make the doors the same size as my

opening in the face frame. This is on purpose. Once my doors are complete, I trim them to size on my jointer, hang the doors in the face frame, then remove the doors and move on to the case.

Build the Case

Begin building the case by gluing up some boards to make the side pieces and shelves. Once those are cut to finished size, cut $\frac{3}{4}$"-wide × $\frac{1}{4}$"-deep dadoes to hold the two fixed shelves in place.

The bottom dado is located $4\frac{3}{4}$" from the bottom edge of the sides. This will make the bottom shelf stick up $\frac{1}{4}$"

above the bottom rail of the face frame and serve as a door stop. The second dado should be flush to the top of the center rail because the drawers will ride on that shelf. Now cut $\frac{1}{2}$" × $\frac{1}{4}$" rabbets in the sides for the back.

Put a bead of glue in the dadoes, then put the shelves in the dadoes and nail the case together through the sides. Some people might wince at nailing a case together this way; I don't. I figure that when the glue finally gives way, as it will someday, the nails will hold the piece together.

Now nail the nailing strip between the sides. The nailing strip should be flush to the top of the sides and $\frac{1}{2}$" in

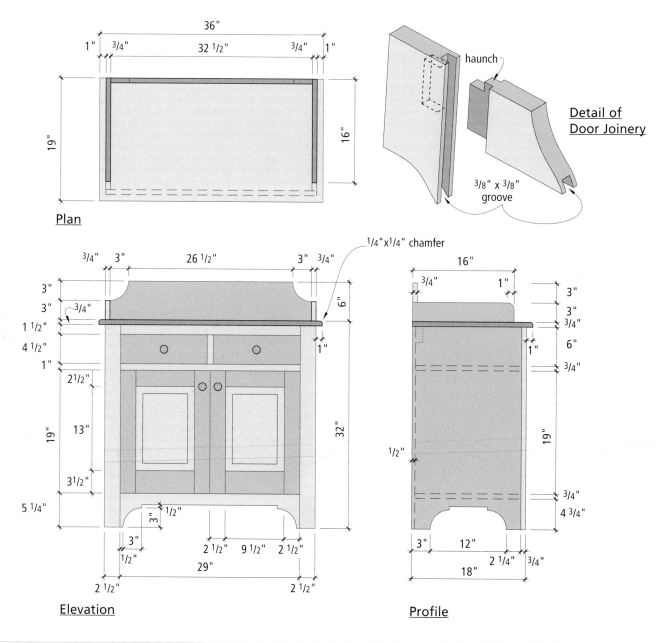

Detail of Door Joinery

Plan

Elevation

Profile

No.	Item	Dimensions T W L	Material	Notes
FACE FRAME				
2	Stiles	¾ x 2½ x 31¼	Maple	
1	Top rail	¾ x 1½ x 31	Maple	1" TBE
1	Bottom rail	¾ x 5¼ x 31	Maple	1" TBE
1	Mid-stile	¾ x 1 x 6½	Maple	1" TBE
1	Mid-rail	¾ x 1 x 31	Maple	1" TBE
CASE				
2	Sides	¾ x 17¼ x 31¼	Maple	
2	Fixed shelves	¾ x 16¾ x 33	Maple	
1	Back	½ x 33 x 31¼	Poplar	shiplapped
1	Top	¾ x 19 x 36	Maple	
1	Splash, back	¾ x 6 x 32½	Maple	3" radius
2	Splash, sides	¾ x 3 x 16	Maple	1" radius
1	Nailing strip	¾ x 1½ x 32½	Poplar	
DOORS				
4	Stiles	¾ x 2½ x 19	Maple	
2	Top rails	¾ x 2½ x 11½	Maple	1" TBE
2	Bottom rails	¾ x 3½ x 11½	Maple	1" TBE
2	Panels	⅝ x 10 x 14	Maple	
DRAWERS				
2	Fronts	¾ x 4⅜ x 13⅞	Maple	
4	Sides	½ x 4⅜ x 17	Poplar	
2	Backs	½ x 3½ x 13⅞	Poplar	
2	Bottoms	½ x 16 x 13⅜	Poplar	

country dry sink **inches**

TBE = Tenon on both ends

No.	Item	Dimensions T W L	Material	Notes
FACE FRAME				
2	Stiles	19 x 64 x 793	Maple	
1	Top rail	19 x 38 x 787	Maple	25mm TBE
1	Bottom rail	19 x 133 x 787	Maple	25mm TBE
1	Mid-stile	19 x 25 x 165	Maple	25mm TBE
1	Mid-rail	19 x 25 x 787	Maple	25mm TBE
CASE				
2	Sides	19 x 438 x 793	Maple	
2	Fixed shelves	19 x 425 x 838	Maple	
1	Back	13 x 838 x 793	Poplar	shiplapped
1	Top	19 x 483 x 914	Maple	
1	Splash, back	19 x 152 x 826	Maple	76mm radius
2	Splash, sides	19 x 76 x 406	Maple	25mm radius
1	Nailing strip	19 x 38 x 826	Poplar	
DOORS				
4	Stiles	19 x 64 x 483	Maple	
2	Top rails	19 x 64 x 292	Maple	25mm TBE
2	Bottom rails	19 x 89 x 292	Maple	25mm TBE
2	Panels	16 x 254 x 356	Maple	
DRAWERS				
2	Fronts	19 x 112 x 352	Maple	
4	Sides	13 x 112 x 432	Poplar	
2	Backs	13 x 89 x 352	Poplar	
2	Bottoms	13 x 406 x 340	Poplar	

country dry sink **millimeters**

TBE = Tenon on both ends

Begin building the top by gluing and nailing the side splash pieces to the back splash pieces. I like to hold the back splash in place using a vise to keep everything in line as it's nailed together.

Now glue and nail the splash pieces to the top. Turn the splash upside down and put a bead of glue on the entire length of the back splash. Then put a bead of glue on the back third of the side splash. If you glue the entire side splash, your top might bust apart after a few seasons.

Place the top on the splash assembly and nail it in place through the underside of the top.

from the back edge of the sides. You'll nail your back to this when the project is complete.

To complete the lower case, glue and nail the face frame to the case. When the glue is dry, cut the shape of the base on the front and sides using a jigsaw. Then clean up your cuts using sandpaper. Now it's time to move on to the top.

Make the Top to Last

There's some cross-grain construction in the top, so you need to be careful about how you put it together to ensure the top doesn't self-destruct.

Begin by gluing up the boards for the top piece, cutting the top to finished size and sanding it to its final grit. Cut a $\frac{1}{4}" \times \frac{1}{4}"$ chamfer on the top edge to soften the edge.

Cut your three splash pieces to size and cut the curved parts. The back splash gets a 3" radius cut on either end. And the side splashes get a 1" radius cut on the front edge as shown in the drawings on page 42. Finish sand all the pieces and follow the instructions under the photos on pages 43 and 44.

Finishing Touches

I make the drawers using half-blind dovetails. I build a simple jig that cranks these out in just a few minutes. See how to build the jig at www.pop-wood.com/features/fea33.html.

To keep the drawers running straight, I nailed in $\frac{3}{4}" \times 1"$ strips of wood on the upper fixed shelf and stops at the back of the case to keep the drawer fronts flush to the front of the case.

The back is made from $\frac{1}{2}"$-thick poplar boards that I shiplap so the edges overlap. I also cut a bead on the shiplapped edges using a beading bit in my router. Fit the back pieces, being sure to leave a gap between each board; don't nail them in place until the dry sink is finished.

Now finish sand all the parts, putty your nail holes and dye the project. I use a diluted red aniline dye, followed by three coats of lacquer.

Now put a bead of glue on the side pieces and top rail of the face frame. The sides will expand and contract the same as the side pieces, so there isn't a cross-grain problem here. Toenail the top into the case piece.

Supplies

Horton Brasses Inc. • 800-754-9127, or www.horton-brasses.com
4 - $1\frac{1}{4}"$ knobs

Woodworker's Supply • 800-645-9292
4 - Amerock adjustable hinges - #891-749

tall
pine clock

Produce a tall pickled
pine clock using simple
tools and off-the-rack
pine boards.

T his tall clock may look
like it was built from
clear pine, which can
run upward of $6 a
board foot (bf), but it
was actually built using #2 grade pon-
derosa pine that went for $1.41 a foot.
And I only pitched 4 of the total 31 bf
I purchased cutting around knots.
When you're on a budget, it pays to
buy smart.

With no jointer or planer in this
shop, I bought nominal 1×12 material
already surfaced on four sides (S4S).
The wide stock meant no edge gluing
was necessary, which saved some time.
In all, you'll need about 18 to 20 hours
to build and finish the clock.

I based my project dimensions on
two factors: the clock's $8\frac{1}{8}$"-diameter
face and the lumber's $11\frac{1}{8}$" net width.
Refer to the Materials List for complete
cutting information.

Build Two Boxes

When you the review the diagram, you'll see the clock's basic elements are an upper and lower box with four vertical supports. Take away the crown and base moulding, and it looks like an oversize box kite.

To begin construction cut out the parts to make the two boxes. No fancy joinery is required, so simply butt joint the parts, fastening them with glue and nails. The sides overlap the front and back. Note that the lower box bottom is inset and the top has a rabbet on four sides to produce a ¼" lip. Leave the lid loose and you have a secret storage compartment! The lid on the upper box is also loose to allow access to the light fixture, while the bottom overlays the four sides.

Before assembling the upper box, cut the holes required for mounting the clock and the recessed light fixture. Center the hole for the light, keeping in mind that the clock hole is centered side to side and 7¼" down from the top of the face. Cutting these holes presented a problem for the tools that I initially purchased for my shop, so an additional expense was required. Did I buy a power jigsaw on a tight budget? Of course not! A narrow-bladed, $9.95 compass saw was the solution. After cutting the holes, assemble the box then presand with 120-grit paper.

Make the Uprights

Make the four legs that tie the two boxes together from two pieces of ¾" material, one 1½" wide and the other ¾" wide. The two pieces are nailed and glued to form an L-shape that's 1½" wide on each outside face. Before joining these pieces, though, two operations are necessary. First, use a sanding block and sand the edge to be joined, eliminating the ragged edge left by the saw. The second operation is to use the table saw to cut the three quirk details on the front face of the uprights.

Lay out and mill these ¹⁄₁₆"-deep details by marking start/stop reference lines on the rip fence which then correspond to reference marks on the back side of the uprights. Start the cut by

Cutting rabbets on the table saw is a two-step process. First, run the part on edge to the depth required. Next lower the blade, reset the fence and run the part flat to cut away the waste.

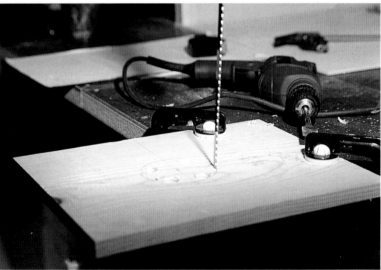

My inexpensive solution to cutting the round cutouts for the clock, light fixture and clock surround moulding is a narrow-bladed compass saw. Before sawing I drilled relief holes.

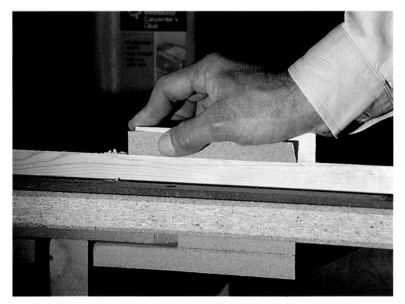

Before gluing and nailing the two-piece uprights, I block sanded the rough edge left by my table saw. The sanding assured the butt joint would seat properly on the mating part.

tall pine clock — inches

No.	Letter	Item	Dimensions T W L	Material
UPPER BOX				
2	A	Front & back	¾ x 10⅝ x 13⅜	Pine
2	B	Sides	¾ x 11⅛ x 13⅜	Pine
2	C	Top & bottom	¾ x 11⅛ x 12⅛	Pine
1	D	Clock surround	¾ x 10⅝ x 7¼	Pine
1	E	Crown mld fnt	¾ x 2½ x 18	Pine
2	F	Crown mld sds	¾ x 2½ x 14½	Pine
1	G	Bot mld fnt	¾ x ¾ x 10⅝	Pine
2	H	Bot mld sds	¾ x ¾ x 9⅝	Pine
BOTTOM BOX				
2	I	Front & back	¾ x 10⅝ x 12	Pine
2	J	Sides	¾ x 11⅛ x 12	Pine
1	K	Bottom	¾ x 11⅛ x 12⅛	Pine
1	L	Top	¾ x 11⅛ x 12⅛	Pine
1	M	Fnt mld/filler	¾ x 3¾ x 10⅝	Pine
2	N	Sds mld/filler	¾ x 3¾ x 9⁷⁄₁₆	Pine
1	O	Base mld fnt	¾ x 3 x 15⅛	Pine
2	P	Base mld sds	¾ x 3 x 13⅜	Pine
LEGS				
4	Q	Uprights	¾ x 1½ x 70	Pine
4	R	Uprights	¾ x ¾ x 70	Pine
3		Tempered Shelves	¼ x 11 x 12	Glass

The clock face was purchased from Klockit, #15140 with Roman dial. For more information, call 800-KLOCKIT.

tall pine clock — millimeters

No.	Letter	Item	Dimensions T W L	Material
UPPER BOX				
2	A	Front & back	19 x 270 x 340	Pine
2	B	Sides	19 x 282 x 340	Pine
2	C	Top & bottom	19 x 282 x 308	Pine
1	D	Clock surround	19 x 270 x 184	Pine
1	E	Crown mld fnt	19 x 64 x 457	Pine
2	F	Crown mld sds	19 x 64 x 369	Pine
1	G	Bot mld fnt	19 x 19 x 270	Pine
2	H	Bot mld sds	19 x 19 x 245	Pine
BOTTOM BOX				
2	I	Front & back	19 x 270 x 305	Pine
2	J	Sides	19 x 282 x 305	Pine
1	K	Bottom	19 x 282 x 308	Pine
1	L	Top	19 x 282 x 308	Pine
1	M	Fnt mld/filler	19 x 95 x 270	Pine
2	N	Sds mld/filler	19 x 95 x 245	Pine
1	O	Base mld fnt	19 x 76 x 384	Pine
2	P	Base mld sds	19 x 76 x 340	Pine
LEGS				
4	Q	Uprights	19 x 38 x 1778	Pine
4	R	Uprights	19 x 19 x 1778	Pine
3		Tempered Shelves	6 x 279 x 305	Glass

The clock face was purchased from Klockit, #15140 with Roman dial. For more information, call 800-KLOCKIT.

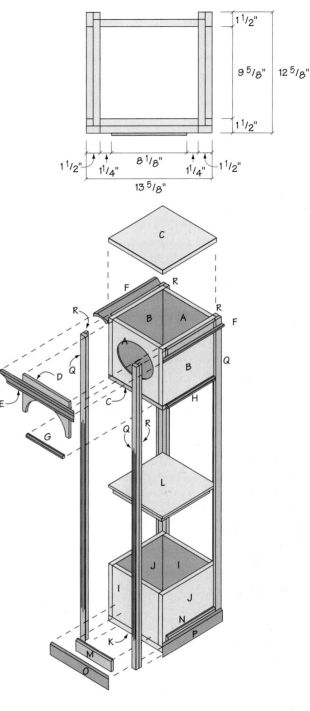

Fence Indexing

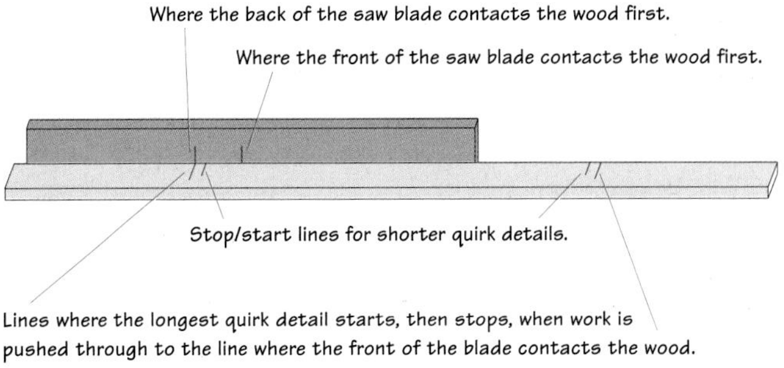

Where the back of the saw blade contacts the wood first.

Where the front of the saw blade contacts the wood first.

Stop/start lines for shorter quirk details.

Lines where the longest quirk detail starts, then stops, when work is pushed through to the line where the front of the blade contacts the wood.

indexing the first layout line on the back of the stock to the line past the blade on the fence. Then slowly lower the stock onto the blade and push the piece through until the opposite layout line matches the line on the fence at the front of the blade. The quirk details used here have a ¼" space between them with the middle one 1½" longer at the top and bottom. With this complete, assemble the legs, then presand them.

Attach the Uprights to the Boxes

This assembly is a breeze. Start by placing the two boxes so they're the proper distance apart and oriented as they should be when assembled. Next, apply glue to the box corner edges and lay the upright in place, making the ends of the upright flush with the top of the upper box and the bottom of the lower one. Now nail the upright to the box. Use the finish nails sparingly and on the side edge only. Continue with this until all four are attached. At this stage the project looks more like a box kite than a clock!

Before applying the mouldings, add filler pieces to the front and sides. These build-up pieces go between the uprights at the top of the upper box and bottom of the lower one. The upper pieces simply back up the crown and give you something to nail to. The lower one projects above the base moulding, providing the additional chamfer detail.

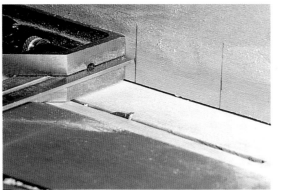

Before running the quirk details, mark the saw fence where the front and back of the blade breaks the plane of the saw table top.

The chamfer detail is cut on the half-circle clock surround moulding by running the part face down on the router table.

Make the Mouldings

Let's begin with the easy mouldings — the chamfer detail. Cut them, with the exception of the clock surround moulding, to width, but wait to cut them to length. The clock surround piece is fit so it's the full width between the uprights and long enough to extend down to the horizontal center of the clock hole. Use the compass saw again and cut out the half circle so a ¼" gap will

The three completed crown moulding parts ready for cutting to length.

be created between the edge of the cutout and clock frame.

With this done, set up your router in a router table with a 45° chamfer bit. I ran the beveled edges on the base moulding, the piece just above the base moulding, the clock surround and the moulding that is applied to the top box's bottom edge. I cut each piece to length, then nailed and glued them in place, mitering the corners of the base moulding.

Now it's time for the most challenging part of the project — making the coved crown moulding and cutting the required compound miters using only the table saw. To mill the cove, first clamp a board at an approximate 33° angle on the saw blade's infeed side. The board serves as a fence to run your stock against as you make the series of shallow cuts that create the cove. Determine the distance of this auxiliary fence to the blade by raising the blade to the highest point of the cut you'll make, about ⅜". Position the fence so the width of the stock is centered on the blade when it passes over it at an angle. When satisfied, run each piece of moulding over the blade, raising the blade about $\frac{1}{16}$" for each pass. When complete, you'll be left with some elbow grease sanding to remove the saw marks, but it's not a terrible task.

To complete the moulding profile remove the temporary angled fence and use the regular fence with the blade tilted to 45°. Cut four beveled edges to produce the finished moulding profile.

To cut the compound miters on the crown's front corners, tilt your saw blade to 30° and set your miter gauge to 35°. To make a right-side miter, set the miter gauge in the slot to the left of the blade. Position the stock face down with the top edge exiting the cut. To make the left miter, move the miter gauge to the right slot, only this time position the stock face up with the top edge leading the cut. When attaching the crown to the project, first nail the front piece after very carefully positioning it not only side-to-side, but also square to both sides. After it's attached, mate the side pieces to it, gluing the miter joint and nailing the sides in place.

Before final sanding and finishing, holes need to be drilled for the wood pegs that support the adjustable glass shelves. To make certain the shelves sit level, I made a simple drilling jig from a piece of scrap material. I also made a simple depth stop to make sure I didn't accidentally drill all the way through the soft pine.

Set all the nail heads and putty them, then sand the project completely using 150-grit paper. Now you're ready for the pickled pine finish. To produce the white effect, use white or off-white latex paint thinned 1 part paint to $1\frac{1}{2}$ parts water. Work one section at a time, using either a brush or rag to apply a modest amount of the thinned paint. Immediately wipe off most of the paint. After it's dry, apply two coats of clear finish over the white, lightly hand sanding between coats with 360-grit paper.

Install the light fixture according to the manufacturer's directions. Make sure you drill vent holes in the back of the upper box near the top to allow heat

The coved crown mould is made using the table saw. Run the stock over the blade at an angle against an auxiliary fence set about 33° askew to the fence.

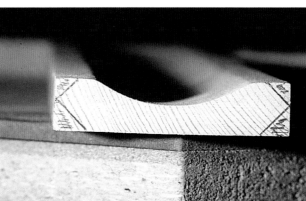

Complete the crown mould profile by making four 45° cuts on the corners of the stock.

The compound miters for the crown mould are cut on the table saw by tilting the blade to 30° and setting the miter gauge to 35°.

Two simple drilling jigs — a piece of wood which fits on the bit, limiting the depth of the hole, and a predrilled plywood template that locates the holes — assure correct location and depth of drilling.

buildup from the fixture to dissipate. Run the plug wire down an outside back leg of the unit, holding it in place with small, insulated "U" nails. I installed an inline switch at a convenient location about midway down for easy on/off control. The clock unit press fits into the hole so it can be removed to adjust the time or replace the battery.

All in all, I concluded that my $73.40 worth of wood, clock and light fixture was a darn good investment. Especially when you compare it with a not too dissimilar unit in the Spiegel catalog for twice the money. It, of course, is smaller, and doesn't have a light, fancy coved crown or quirk details, either!

hanging
china cupboard

The perfect place to store and display your everyday
china so it's at arm's length when dinnertime comes.

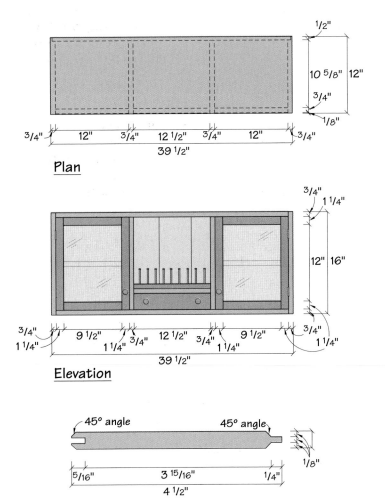

Plan

Elevation

45° angle   45° angle

1/8"

5/16"   3 15/16"   1/4"

4 1/2"

Detail of back piece

If you want to show off your
dinnerware, glass doors and
open shelving, you can do a
better job than standard
kitchen cabinets. Rather than
remodeling your kitchen, add this
hanging cupboard to your dining area.

I chose ash because its light color
complements the cabinet's open design.
Begin construction by gluing up any
panels you might need. When the glue
is dry and the panels have been sanded
or planed flat, cut them to finished
size. Then cut a $1/2$" $\times$ $1/2$" rabbet on the
back edge of the top and bottom
pieces, and the same size stopped rabbet on the sides. Next mark the horizontal divider, vertical divider, sides,
top and bottom for biscuits to hold the
case together. Cut the slots and assemble the case by first gluing the horizontal divider in place between the two
vertical dividers. Then glue this assembly in place between the top and bottom, flushing it to the inside of the
back rabbet. Finally glue the sides on.

Next cut the pieces necessary to
form the $3/8$"-thick back. The diagram
at left shows a detail of the back.

When the glue is dry, chisel out the corners of the back rabbet, then fit the back. The tongue-and-groove joint allows the solid back to move with humidity changes, so leave a little room between each piece. Don't permanently attach the back pieces until the cabinet is finished.

With the carcass complete, cut the pieces for the door stiles and rails. I used $\frac{1}{4}$" × $\frac{1}{2}$"-long stub tenon joinery on the doors, cutting the groove in the stiles the full length. After the doors are assembled, use a $\frac{1}{2}$" rabbeting bit in a router table to cut the back side off the groove in the stiles, forming a rabbet to accept the glass panes. Now cut the same rabbet in the rails.

Next build the drawer. I used a tongue-and-rabbet joint to attach the front to the sides, and a simple rabbet joint for the back piece. Tack the bottom in place in a $\frac{3}{16}$" × $\frac{1}{4}$" rabbet on the bottom of the four drawer pieces.

Make the two plate holders, which consist of wood strips with store-bought necktie hangers glued into holes spaced $1\frac{1}{4}$" apart. Now check the fit of the doors and drawer. I held the doors and drawer $\frac{1}{8}$" in from the front edge of the cabinet.

Drill shelf pin holes for the shelves, and add a stop block at the rear of the drawer cavity to hold the drawer $\frac{1}{8}$" in from the front. The piece is ready to finish.

After the finish is dry, permanently attach the back. I used a single nail centered on each piece — top and bottom — to hold the back in place and allow the pieces to expand. To hang this somewhat heavy cabinet on the wall directly through the back, I reinforced two of the back pieces with $1\frac{1}{4}$" screws. Next put the glass in the frames and pin $\frac{1}{4}$" × $\frac{1}{4}$" ash strips behind the glass to hold it in place.

Screw the plate holders in position, checking the spacing between the two rails to hold your plates slightly above the surface of the cabinet. The last step is to mount the doors, then add door and drawer knobs and a couple of door catches.

With the cabinet hung in a place of honor, the rest is a matter of deciding which plates and glasses will go on display.

Supplies

Rockler • 800-279-4441,
or www.rockler.com
4 - Non-mortise hinges - #28712
4 - Sash knobs - #36459
18 - Necktie pegs - #21980
2 - Brass ball catches - #28613
8 - Shelf pins - #30437

hanging china cupboard **inches**

No.	Item	Dimensions T W L	Material
2	Sides	$\frac{3}{4}$ x 12 x 16	Ash
2	Top & bot	$\frac{3}{4}$ x 12 x 38	Ash
2	Vertical dividers	$\frac{3}{4}$ x $11\frac{1}{2}$ x $14\frac{1}{2}$	Ash
1	Horizontal divider	$\frac{3}{4}$ x $11\frac{1}{2}$ x $12\frac{1}{2}$	Ash
2	Shelves	$\frac{3}{4}$ x $10\frac{1}{2}$ x $11\frac{7}{8}$	Ash
4	Door stiles	$\frac{3}{4}$ x $1\frac{1}{4}$ x $14\frac{1}{2}$	Ash
4	Door rails	$\frac{3}{4}$ x $1\frac{1}{4}$ x $10\frac{1}{2}$	Ash
1	Drawer front	$\frac{3}{4}$ x $2\frac{1}{2}$ x $12\frac{1}{2}$	Ash
2	Plate supports	$\frac{5}{8}$ x $\frac{3}{4}$ x $12\frac{3}{8}$	Ash
2	Drawer sides	$\frac{1}{2}$ x $2\frac{1}{2}$ x $10\frac{1}{4}$	Ash
1	Drawer back	$\frac{1}{2}$ x $2\frac{1}{2}$ x $12\frac{1}{8}$	Ash
1	Drawer bot	$\frac{1}{4}$ x $10\frac{1}{4}$ x $11\frac{7}{8}$	Ply
9	Back pieces	$\frac{3}{8}$ x $4\frac{1}{2}$ x $15\frac{1}{2}$	Ash
2	Glass panes	$\frac{1}{8}$ x $10\frac{3}{8}$ x $12\frac{3}{4}$	
18	Tie hangers	$\frac{1}{4}$ x 3	

hanging china cupboard **millimeters**

No.	Item	Dimensions T W L	Material
2	Sides	19 x 305 x 406	Ash
2	Top & bot	19 x 305 x 965	Ash
2	Vertical dividers	19 x 292 x 369	Ash
1	Horizontal divider	19 x 292 x 318	Ash
2	Shelves	19 x 267 x 301	Ash
4	Door stiles	19 x 32 x 369	Ash
4	Door rails	19 x 32 x 267	Ash
1	Drawer front	19 x 64 x 318	Ash
2	Plate supports	16 x 19 x 315	Ash
2	Drawer sides	13 x 64 x 260	Ash
1	Drawer back	13 x 64 x 308	Ash
1	Drawer bot	6 x 260 x 301	Ply
9	Back pieces	10 x 115 x 394	Ash
2	Glass panes	3 x 264 x 318	
18	Tie hangers	6 x 76	

stacking
storage boxes

Solve all your clutter problems with these modular and amazingly simple drop-front crates.

In any workshop, efficient storage is very important, especially if your workshop space is at a premium. These storage boxes can snuggle up against a wall in an otherwise unused corner of your workshop. They are good, solid boxes that you can tote from one place to another. And unlike most storage boxes once these are stacked you still have access to the contents of the lower boxes.

Assemble the ends by placing a 5½"-wide end piece in the middle of two 3½" end pieces. Separate them slightly by placing a business card between each piece at the top and bottom. Offset the middle piece ¾" higher than the two side pieces, using a scrap piece of wood as a guide. This "notch" is used to lock the storage boxes together when they are stacked. Screw two battens to the ends so they are flush to the front and back edges, and even with the top and bottom of the 3½"-wide pieces.

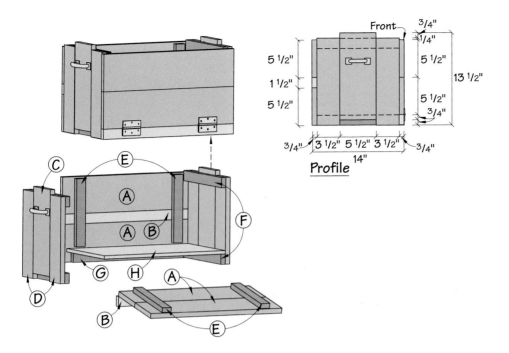

Back Pieces

For the backs, screw a bottom ledger onto one 5½"-wide side piece so it is centered and flush with the bottom edge. Then, lay out first a 1½"-wide piece and another 5½"-wide piece, and screw the three together using two battens. The battens are held ¼" down from the top and 2" in from the ends.

Doors

To make the doors, use two 5½"-wide pieces and attach the battens ¼" from the top and 2" from the ends. Screw the bottom ledger to the 1½"-wide front piece, flush to the top and bottom and centered end to end. Place the two front parts face up and attach the hinges.

Assembly

Glue and screw the back to the outside of the ends, then glue and screw the lower front to the ends. Finally screw the bottom in place, making sure it rests on the ledgers on all sides.

Finish

The door is held closed by eye hooks attached at the ends, and handles are screwed to both ends of the box. You can leave the box natural if desired, or give it two light coats of polyurethane varnish for extra protection.

stacking storage boxes		**inches**		
No.	Ltr.	Item	Dimensions T W L	Material
4	A	Back & door pieces	¾ × 5½ × 22	Pine
2	B	Back & front pieces	¾ × 1½ × 22	Pine
2	C	End pieces	¾ × 5½ × 12¾	Pine
4	D	End pieces	¾ × 3½ × 12¾	Pine
4	E	Back & door battens	¾ × 1½ × 10	Pine
4	F	End battens	¾ × 1½ × 12½	Pine
2	G	Bottom ledgers	¾ × 1½ × 19	Pine
1	H	Bottom	½ × 12½ × 20½	Plywood

stacking storage boxes		**millimeters**		
No.	Ltr.	Item	Dimensions T W L	Material
4	A	Back & door pieces	19 × 140 × 559	Pine
2	B	Back & front pieces	19 × 38 × 559	Pine
2	C	End pieces	19 × 140 × 324	Pine
4	D	End pieces	19 × 89 × 324	Pine
4	E	Back & door battens	19 × 38 × 254	Pine
4	F	End battens	19 × 38 × 318	Pine
2	G	Bottom ledgers	19 × 38 × 483	Pine
1	H	Bottom	13 × 318 × 521	Plywood

storage &
assembly bench

When space is tight (and when isn't it?), you'll appreciate this modular system which gives you a height-adjustable assembly bench, two stands for benchtop tools and six drawers of roll-around storage. Best of all, it breaks down fast and stores in small spaces.

My shop at home is a two-car garage. To make things more complicated, my wife feels pretty strongly that the two cars should be allowed to stay in the garage. What a silly idea, but it's been an interesting challenge to keep her happy and still work comfortably on my projects. At the heart of this dilemma is getting enough storage and assembly space. There's enough room in the garage to put some shallow cabinets on or against the walls, but storing my "assembly bench" (fold-up horses, planks and a partial sheet of plywood) stops me from getting to my storage. And while the fold-up horses are handy, they're not as stable as I'd prefer and I can't adjust them higher or lower. Sometimes I want to work 24" off the ground, other times 34". I decided it was time to solve my dilemma, and this project is the result. When assembled, this unit offers sturdy, adjustable-height bench space with easy access to the stuff in the drawers. When not in use, the two cabinets store conveniently against the wall. You also can use them as benchtop tool stands and still have easy access to the drawers.

Building Boxes

This is a basic project. The only complicated part is the height-adjustment feature of the cabinets. I haven't spent a lot of time illustrating the cabinet construction, but the illustrations and the construction description should get you there safely.

The cabinets consist of a ¾"-thick plywood top and bottom, rabbeted between the two ¾"-thick sides. The back is also ¾" and is rabbeted into the sides, top and bottom. Start by cutting the pieces to size, then cut ½" × ¾" rabbets on the top, back and bottom inside edge of each side. I made the rabbets on my table saw, but you could easily use a router instead. Then cut the same rabbet on the back edge of the top and bottom pieces.

I used my 2" brad nailer to shoot the cases together, adding some glue to the joint for good measure. Screws (#8 × 1¼") would also do the job here. Use the backs to square up the cabinets. This will be important when you install the drawers.

I was feeling pretty minimalist with this project and decided to let the utility show through by simply rounding over all the plywood edges with a ¼" roundover bit in my router. If you prefer a more finished appearance, take the extra time to apply iron-on veneer tape to the exposed plywood edges.

To make adding the height-adjustable supports easier, I attached the four casters — two standard, non-swivel and two swivel-locking — to the cabinets at this time.

Going Up, Going Down

I went through a lot of different ideas to make the top height-adjustable. After making it a lot more complicated than necessary, I threw away those drawings and went back to simple. The height-adjustable table supports are brought to you by the letters "U" and "L." The support arms are U-shaped solid birch assemblies that slip into two L-shaped channels on each side of the cabinets.

Start by jointing and thicknessing all the solid birch necessary for the pieces and cut them to finished size, except for the channel pieces. Leave those pieces a little long until after they're glued up. I once again took advantage of my brad nailer to speed up the assembly process. Glue and nail the channel fronts to the channel sides, then set everything aside to let the glue cure.

While they're drying, cut the channel bottoms to length. Cut an extra one to use as a spacer while you're at it. When the channels are ready, clean up any extra glue, then get the roundover bit out again. I rounded all the outside surfaces on the channels and the top

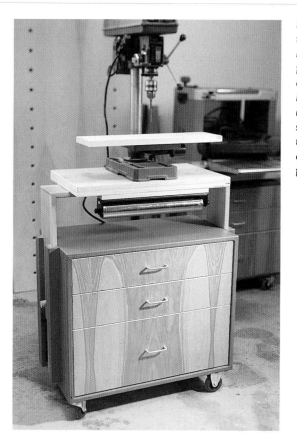

By adding smaller tops to the individual cabinets, each makes a fine tool stand with lots of storage beneath. Note the roller stand mounted on the underside of the top. Flip the top over and you've created an outfeed table for any machine.

I used my brad nailer to tack the channel bottom in place between the two channels through the front and through the sides. Be careful not to shoot too close to the end of a piece to avoid blowouts.

lips where the support arms will enter the channels.

Glue and nail the channel assemblies together, using the extra bottom to help maintain even spacing at the top of the assembly.

To attach the channels to the cabinets, first use a combination square to make a line 4⅛" in from the front and back edges of each cabinet. Double-check the lines to make sure they will fall in the exact center of each of the channel sides. After checking, drill five

evenly spaced 3⁄16" clearance holes on each line. Countersink each hole from the inside of the cabinets, then attach the channel assemblies to the cabinets, holding the top of the channel flush to the cabinet top.

Now move to the support arms themselves. Use your drill press to make a 1"-diameter hole through each support arm, 3" up from the bottom edge and centered on the piece. On each cabinet, mark the location for five 1" holes centered on the spaces be-

After drilling the clearance holes in the cabinet sides, I used a clamp to hold the channel assembly in place while pilot drilling, then screwing the channels in place from the inside of the cabinet.

tween the channels, locating the first 6" up from the inside of the channel bottom, then 2" on center from that first mark. These holes shouldn't be drilled all the way through the cabinet side or the dowels will interfere with the drawers. Make the holes about ⅝" deep. I used a Forstner bit and used the spur tip as an indicator of depth. By drilling slowly I was able to tell when the spur poked through on the inside, and stop the hole at that depth.

Next, round over all the edges on the support arms except those on the top, then slip the arms into the channels and check the fit. If they don't move easily (though they shouldn't be too loose) adjust the fit. With the arms all the way down in the channel, take one of the top plates and lay it across the two arms. Mark the location of the arms on the top plate, allowing the arms to naturally settle in the channels. If they're pushed too tightly to the cabinet, the arms won't move easily.

Head to the table saw and cut ½"-deep rabbets on each end of the top plate using the marks for the support arms to determine the width. Then drill

storage & assembly bench — inches

No.	Item	Dimensions T W L	Material	Notes
CABINETS				
4	Sides	¾ x 15 x 21¾	Birch ply	½ x ¾ rabbets, 3 sides
4	Tops & bots	¾ x 15 x 27	Birch ply	½ x ¾ rabbet, back
2	Backs	¾ x 27 x 21¼	Birch ply	
2	Tops	¾ x 30 x 72	Birch ply	
4	Support arms	¾ x 6 x 19⅝	Birch	
2	Top plates	⅞ x 6 x 29⅛	Birch	½ x ¾ rabbets, ends
8	Channel sides	¾ x ⅞ x 20	Birch	
8	Channel fronts	¾ x 2 x 20	Birch	
4	Channel bots	¾ x ⅞ x 6	Birch	
4	Dowels	1 x 2½	Maple	
4	Dowels	¾ x 1⅝	Maple	
DRAWERS				
4	Fronts	¾ x 5 x 25⅞	Birch ply	clearance space incl.
2	Fronts	¾ x 10 x 25⅞	Birch ply	clearance space incl.
8	Box sides	½ x 4 x 13¼	Birch ply	¼ x ¼ groove, 3 sides
4	Box sides	½ x 9 x 13¼	Birch ply	¼ x ¼ groove, 3 sides
4	Box fronts	½ x 4 x 24½	Birch ply	¼ x ¼ tongue, ends
4	Box backs	½ x 3½ x 24½	Birch ply	¼ x ¼ tongue, ends
2	Box fronts	½ x 9 x 24½	Birch ply	¼ x ¼ tongue, ends
2	Box backs	½ x 8½ x 24½	Birch ply	¼ x ¼ tongue, ends
6	Bottoms	¼ x 13 x 24⁵⁄₁₆	Ply	

storage & assembly bench — millimeters

No.	Item	Dimensions T W L	Material	Notes
CABINETS				
4	Sides	19 x 381 x 552	Birch ply	13 x 19 rabbets, 3 sides
4	Tops & bots	19 x 381 x 686	Birch ply	13 x 19 rabbet, back
2	Backs	19 x 686 x 539	Birch ply	
2	Tops	19 x 762 x 1829	Birch ply	
4	Support arms	19 x 152 x 499	Birch	
2	Top plates	22 x 152 x 740	Birch	13 x 19 rabbets, ends
8	Channel sides	19 x 22 x 508	Birch	
8	Channel fronts	19 x 51 x 508	Birch	
4	Channel bots	19 x 22 x 152	Birch	
4	Dowels	25 x 64	Maple	
4	Dowels	19 x 41	Maple	
DRAWERS				
4	Fronts	19 x 127 x 657	Birch ply	clearance space incl.
2	Fronts	19 x 254 x 657	Birch ply	clearance space incl.
8	Box sides	13 x 102 x 336	Birch ply	6 x 6 groove, 3 sides
4	Box sides	13 x 229 x 336	Birch ply	6 x 6 groove, 3 sides
4	Box fronts	13 x 102 x 623	Birch ply	6 x 6 tongue, ends
4	Box backs	13 x 89 x 623	Birch ply	6 x 6 tongue, ends
2	Box fronts	13 x 229 x 623	Birch ply	6 x 6 tongue, ends
2	Box backs	13 x 216 x 623	Birch ply	6 x 6 tongue, ends
6	Bottoms	6 x 330 x 618	Ply	

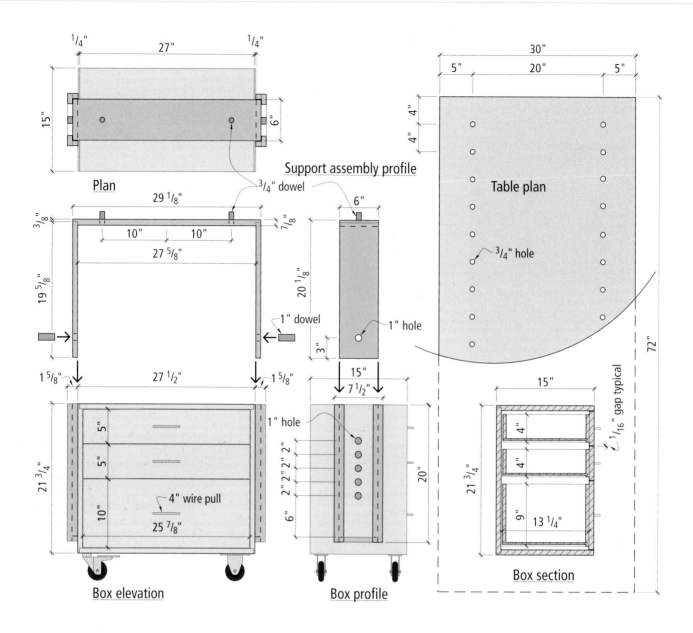

Plan

Support assembly profile

Table plan

Box elevation

Box profile

Box section

clearance holes and screw the top plates to the support arms after pilot drilling the hole to avoid splitting.

You should be able to raise and lower the entire assembly with little resistance. I used simple dowels to lock the arms at whatever height I wanted. Round over the edges of the top plate, then move on to building the benchtop.

More Than an Assembly Top

The top is made from two ¾"-thick pieces of plywood glued together. Spread glue thinly over the entire surface of one piece, then nail the corners to keep the top from slipping around while you clamp up the top "sandwich."

To give the top even more versatility, I added dog holes along the front and back edge to accommodate a set of Veritas Bench Pups and Wonder Pups. These work like vises and can hold almost any workpiece. These holes also become the attachment points to hold the top in place on the cabinets.

Locate the dog holes 5" in from each edge and spaced 4" on center, starting 4" from either end. I used a ¾" auger bit to make the holes, and the photo on page 59 shows a jig I used to make sure the holes are straight.

With the holes drilled, mark a center line down the length of each support top plate. Then lay the benchtop on

top of the cabinets and position it evenly on the top plates. Now look through a set of dog holes in the benchtop and move things around until the center line on the plate is in the center of the holes. Use a pencil to mark the hole locations on the top plate, then remove the top.

Drill ¾"-diameter holes partway through the top plates (⅝" deep). Then drill a 3/16" clearance hole the rest of the way through the plates, centered on the holes, countersinking the holes from the underside of the top plate. Cut four ¾"-diameter dowels to 1⅝" in length, and screw them in these holes from the underside of the top plates.

The top can now be easily located on the dowels without having to bend over. Once in place, the dowels hold the cabinets in place, and make the entire bench more sturdy. But don't forget to round everything over. Not only did I round the top's edges, but I also rounded the lips of the dog holes. This makes it easier to locate the dowels and dogs and also keeps the plywood from splintering at the sharp edges.

Sturdy Storage Drawers

The drawers are the last step and are designed for basic utility. They are ½" plywood boxes with ¼"-thick plywood bottoms and a ¾" false front. I used tongue-and-groove joinery on the drawer boxes.

Set up either a ¼" stack dado in your table saw, or a ¼" bit in your router table. Then set the fence to leave ¼" between the fence and bit or blade. Set the depth of the cut for ¼", then run the front, back and bottom inside edges of each drawer side. Also run the bottom inside edge of each drawer front.

Next adjust the fence on your saw/router table to cut the tongues on the drawer fronts and back. Check the fit, then run all the fronts and backs. The drawers are then glued and nailed together. The bottoms slip into the groove in the sides and front, and then are nailed in place to the bottom edge of the drawer back. Use the bottoms to make sure the drawers are square before nailing them in place.

The false drawer fronts are again simple and utilitarian: ¾" plywood with the edges rounded over. I held each drawer box ¼" up from the bottom edge of each front. Attach the drawer handles — simple 4" chrome pulls from almost any home center that cost about $2 each — to the fronts, countersinking the screw heads flush to the back of the drawer fronts. The false fronts are screwed in place through the drawer box fronts. Mount the slides following the hardware instructions.

I added a couple coats of paint to the cabinets, but left the top as bare wood. I added a coat of lacquer to the

A 1" dowel is a simple and secure way to hold the support arms at the proper height. The five hole locations, and the all-the-way-down position, give you a variety of working heights.

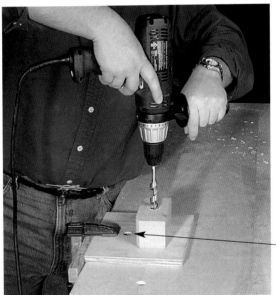

The drilling jig is simply a piece of plywood with an edge stop (like a bench hook) with a guiding block screwed in position over the hole (centered 5" from the edge). You'll notice another hole drilled through the plywood in front of the block. That hole is in line with the guiding hole and lets you see your positioning line drawn on the top to know if you're in the correct location to drill.

ALIGNMENT HOLE

top support assembly and the drawer fronts. There's only one thing left to do to make these storage cabinets all they can be. Make a couple of auxiliary tops to fit on the individual cabinets. I made mine with a piece of ¾" plywood, drilled to match the dowels. Add a roller and you have a height-adjustable outfeed table that can be used with your table saw, jointer, planer or any other machine. When not in use as a bench or outfeed table, you have two handy tool stands that tuck away against the wall — right next to the cars.

Supplies

Grizzly Industrial, Inc. • 800-523-4777, or www.grizzly.com
4 - 3" fixed casters - #H0689
4 - 3" swivel casters w/brake - #H0693
6 - 12" full-extension slides - #H2902

Lee Valley • 800-871-8158, or www.leevalley.com
2 - Wonder Pups - #05G10.02
1 - Bench Pups - #05G04.04

shaker
firewood box

This faithful reproduction
is a one-weekend wonder.

If you haven't already stumbled on the concept of storing a larger cache of logs indoors, this Shaker reproduction will provide a stylish location for your wood stash.

Using pine, the piece is simple enough to complete in a weekend. First cut all of your pieces to length and plane them down to $^3/_4$" thickness. You'll almost certainly end up having to glue up some boards to attain the $20^3/_4$" width. We opted to use biscuits to align the boards during the glue-up process.

Once the glue is dry, move to the next step — sizing the boards according to the Materials List. Because you're working with a fairly plain wood and design, the attention you give to grain figure and to matching wood color will make the piece more dramatic.

The next step is to lay out and cut the radius on the top front corner of each side. Use the profile view to locate the beginning and ending points of the radius. Use trammel points set at a

$10^1/_2$" radius to mark the corner, then use a jigsaw to cut both sides. Cut to the outside of the mark, allowing about $^1/_{16}$" overage to be sanded off. Clamp the two sides together for a final sanding to make sure the two radii match.

The next step involves cutting rabbets. We used two processes for this step. For the $^3/_4$" × $^1/_2$" rabbets we used the table saw, first running the $^3/_4$" dimension with the piece flat to the table, then the $^1/_2$" dimension with the piece on edge. Make sure your waste falls away from the fence to avoid binding between the fence and blade.

After making all the necessary $^3/_4$" × $^1/_2$" rabbets, set up a router with a $^1/_2$" × $^1/_2$" rabbeting bit with a pilot bearing. Use this setup to run the necessary rabbets to accept the back pieces.

If you haven't already done so, run the six back panels down to $^1/_2$" thick and cut to finished size. Then adjust the router setup to cut a $^1/_2$" × $^1/_4$" rabbet on opposing long edges of the back panels. These rabbets will give a

The $^1/_4$" spacing shown on the back panels is accomplished by rabbeting a $^1/_4$" × $^1/_2$" rabbet on opposing long edges.

shiplapped detail to the back of the box and also allow for expansion of the boards left to right.

The next setup for your router uses the rounded portion of a Roman ogee bit to run a cove profile on the radiused side edges.

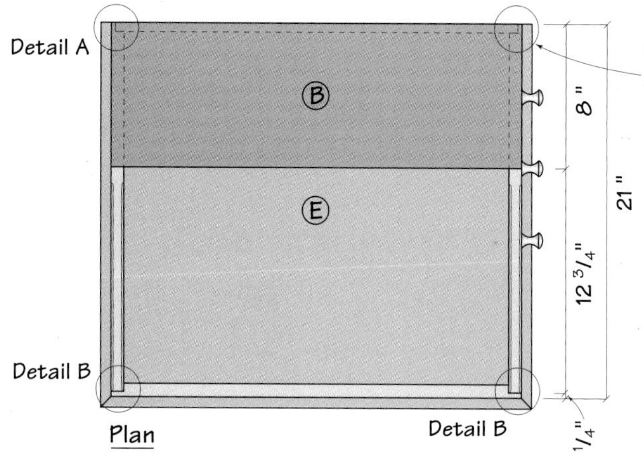
Detail A
Detail A
Detail B
Detail B
8"
12 3/4"
21"
1/4"
Plan

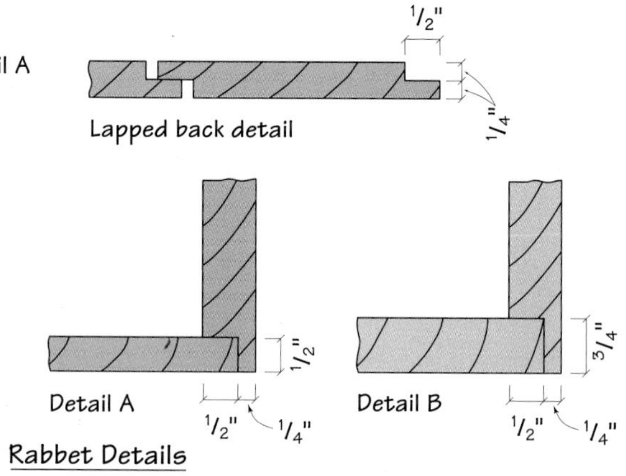
1/2"
1/4"
Lapped back detail
1/2"
3/4"
Detail A
Detail B
1/2"
1/4"
1/2"
1/4"
Rabbet Details

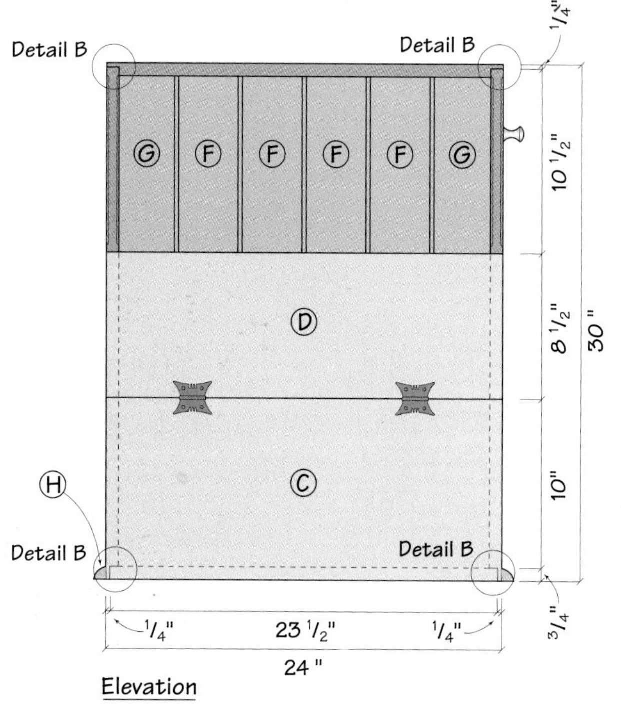
Detail B
Detail B
1/4"
10 1/2"
8 1/2"
30"
10"
3/4"
Detail B
Detail B
1/4"
23 1/2"
1/4"
24"
Elevation

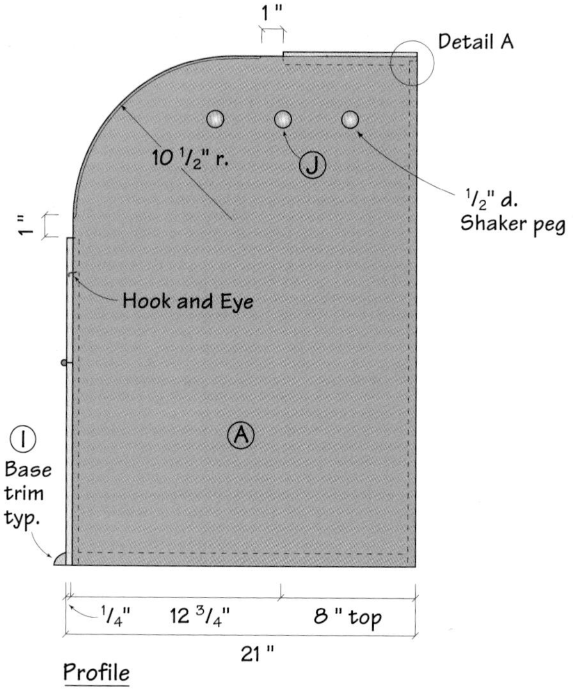
1"
Detail A
10 1/2" r.
1/2" d.
Shaker peg
1"
Hook and Eye
Base
trim
typ.
1/4"
12 3/4"
8" top
21"
Profile

shaker firewood box inches

LOW BOOKCASE

No.	Ltr.	Item	Dimensions (inches) T W L
2	A	Sides	3/4 x 20 3/4 x 29 3/4
1	B	Top	3/4 x 8 x 24
1	C	Front	3/4 x 10 x 24
1	D	Door	3/4 x 8 1/2 x 24
1	E	Bottom	3/4 x 20 x 23 1/2
4	F	Back panels	1/2 x 4 3/16 x 29 3/4
2	G	Back panels	1/2 x 3 7/16 x 29 3/4
2	H	Base trim	1/2 x 1 x 21 5/8
1	I	Base trim	1/2 x 1 x 24 1/4
3	J	Wooden knobs	1/2 x 1 1/4

shaker firewood box millimeters

LOW BOOKCASE

No.	Ltr.	Item	Dimensions T W L
2	A	Sides	19 x 527 x 756
1	B	Top	19 x 203 x 610
1	C	Front	19 x 254 x 610
1	D	Door	19 x 216 x 610
1	E	Bottom	19 x 508 x 597
4	F	Back panels	13 x 107 x 756
2	G	Back panels	13 x 87 x 756
2	H	Base trim	13 x 25 x 549
1	I	Base trim	13 x 25 x 616
3	J	Wooden knobs	13 x 32

I used a ⅛" roundover bit to soften the perimeter edges of the door and front (don't round over the mating edges) as well as the front and sides of the top.

Before assembly, take the time to finish sand all the interior and any surfaces that will be difficult to sand after assembly. You will also want to sand off any glue or board-matching irregularities at this time.

Assemble the box using 1¼" finish nails. Start by attaching the bottom between the two sides, flushing up the front edges of all three pieces. Use the top to help establish the spacing while nailing the sides. Next flush the top to the rear edge and nail it in place.

Now that you've established the box, nail the front into place across the bottom edge, check for square and nail up the sides.

The next step is to nail the back in place. You'll need to pay particular attention to spacing the back pieces to maintain a uniform spacing on the shiplap joints.

To add another detail to the box we used a simple ¾" roundover bit to detail the top edge of the base trim pieces. We then mitered the front corners and tacked the trim into place.

Mark the locations for the hanging pegs, drill your holes and glue the pegs into place. Be aware of glue squeeze-out or it will show when you put the finish on.

Now sand the entire piece to get it ready for finishing. We opted for a simple coat of clear lacquer to show the natural beauty of the sugar pine while sealing and protecting the wood.

Once the finish has hardened it's time to put on the hardware. To keep with the traditional styling of the firewood box, I went with wrought-iron butterfly hinges. The hardware shown was found at a local specialty hardware store, but you'll find similar pieces at the stores mentioned on the supplies list at the right.

Once the hardware's in place, the only detail left is stocking the box with wood. Then settle down for the evening in front of a cozy fire.

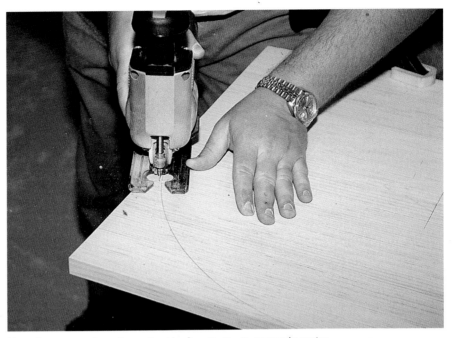

Use a jigsaw to cut the radius on the sides. Pay attention to tear-out by cutting from the inside of each piece.

By using a portion of a Roman ogee bit, a delicate detail is added to the radiused edges of the sides. A cove bit with a guide bearing will also work.

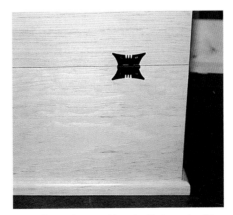

The simple addition of a base shoe moulding helps make the piece more pleasing to the eye.

Supplies

Paxton Hardware Co. • 410-592-8505

Horton Brasses Inc. • 800-754-9127, or www.horton-brasses.com

Ball and Ball • 800-257-3711, or www.ballandball-us.com

Wrought-iron hinges add to the Shaker style of the piece and complete the reproduction look.

asian
bedside table

This frame and panel project is all about grooves, tongues and ancient proverbs.

uilding cabinetry can give you a serious case of Zen Buddhism. In fact, the contradictions in woodworking are sometimes amusing — if not enlightening. Cabinets, for the most part, are more air than wood. To build a piece of furniture is mostly a process of removing wood. And to make a project look as simple and plain as this one does is quite a complicated process.

Now before you start worrying that this simple bedside table is too much for your woodworking skills, remember my favorite Bulgarian proverb: "If you wish to drown, do not torture yourself with shallow water."

Frames and Panels

Except for two small pieces of plywood in the sliding doors, this project is made entirely out of solid wood. To account for the seasonal expansion and contraction of the material, the table is built using a series of frame and panel

assemblies. In a nutshell, all of the frames are connected using mortise-and-tenon joinery. The panels all rest in $\frac{3}{8}$"-wide × $\frac{3}{8}$"-deep grooves in the frames. After you have milled all the parts using the Materials List and glued up any panels you might need, I recommend you begin by building the doors.

Lightweight but Solid
Sliding Doors

The sliding doors on this table run in $\frac{1}{4}$"-wide × $\frac{1}{4}$"-deep grooves cut into the frame pieces. Once this table is glued up, the doors are in there for good. Or, you can easily make the doors removable by shortening the tongue on the top of the doors and doing a little sanding. To ensure the doors slide smoothly for years to come, choose straight-grained stock for the parts.

The rails and stiles of the doors are joined using mortises and tenons. The plywood panel rests in a rabbet cut in the back of the door, and the slats are merely glued onto the panel.

We shape clay into a pot, but it is the emptiness inside that holds whatever we want.

— LAO TZU, ZEN SAYING

Begin by cutting your $\frac{1}{4}$"-thick × 1"-long tenons on the rails. As you can see in the photos at the right, the shoulders facing the outside edges of the door are $\frac{1}{2}$" bigger than the ones facing inside. This makes a cleaner-looking joint when you cut the tongue on the top and bottom of the door. Now cut the matching mortises in the stiles. Glue and clamp the doors.

When the glue is dry, cut a $\frac{1}{4}$"-deep × $\frac{3}{8}$"-wide rabbet on the back side of each door. Square the corners with a chisel. Finish sand the $\frac{1}{4}$" birch plywood panel and then glue it in the rabbet. When that glue is dry, glue the slats in place spaced 1" apart.

To complete the doors, cut a $\frac{1}{4}$"-thick × $\frac{3}{8}$"-long tongue on the top and bottom edge of the back side of the doors.

The Case

Begin work on the case by cutting $\frac{1}{2}$"-thick × 1"-long tenons on all the rails with a $\frac{1}{4}$" shoulder all around. Now use your tenons to lay out the locations of the mortises on the legs. You want all of your rails to be set back $\frac{1}{8}$" from the outside edge of the legs.

The only anomaly comes when laying out the mortises for the beefy front bottom rail. Its mortises run vertically instead of horizontally.

Cut the $1\frac{1}{16}$"-deep mortises. I used a hollow-chisel mortiser equipped with a $\frac{1}{2}$" bit. As you'll see when you get into it, cutting these mortises is a bit different than in most case work. You'll clamp your work to your mortiser's fence, then move the fence in and out to cut the mortises, except when cutting the mortises for the front bottom rail, which are cut conventionally. Then miter the tenons so they fit in the mortises without bumping into each other.

You can see the large shoulder on the door tenon here as I'm dry fitting the door. The large shoulder makes for a cleaner-looking tongue.

MOVE DOOR IN THIS DIRECTION

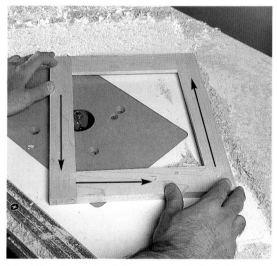

I should install a starting pin in my router table for making cuts like these. If you take it slow and steady you shouldn't have any problems. Make sure you cut against the rotation of the cutter.

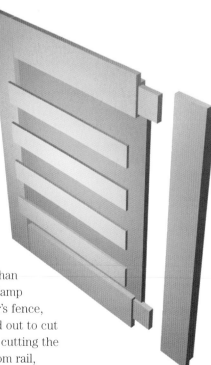

asian bedside table inches

TOP

No.	Item	Dimensions T W L	Material	Comments
2	Top stiles	$1^{3}/_{4}$ x $1^{3}/_{4}$ x 30	Maple	$^{3}/_{8}$" x $^{3}/_{8}$" groove on inside edge
2	Top rails	$1^{3}/_{4}$ x $1^{3}/_{4}$ x 18	Maple	1" TBE, $^{3}/_{8}$" x $^{3}/_{8}$" groove on inside edge
1	Panel	$^{3}/_{4}$ x $16^{1}/_{2}$ x $20^{1}/_{2}$	Maple	in $^{3}/_{8}$" x $^{3}/_{8}$" groove; $^{1}/_{2}$" x $^{3}/_{8}$" rabbet, all sides

BASE

No.	Item	Dimensions T W L	Material	Comments
4	Legs	$1^{3}/_{4}$ x $1^{3}/_{4}$ x 23	Maple	$^{3}/_{8}$" x $^{3}/_{8}$" groove for side & back panels
4	Rails for sides	1 x $1^{1}/_{2}$ x 14	Maple	1" TBE, $^{3}/_{8}$" x $^{3}/_{8}$" groove for side panels
3	Rails frt & bk	1 x $1^{1}/_{2}$ x 22	Maple	1" TBE, $^{3}/_{8}$" x $^{3}/_{8}$" groove for back panel
1	Front bottom rail	2 x $1^{1}/_{2}$ x 22	Maple	1" TBE
2	Top & bot panels	$^{3}/_{4}$ x $12^{3}/_{4}$ x $20^{3}/_{4}$	Maple	$^{1}/_{2}$" x $^{3}/_{8}$" rabbet on edges; rests in $^{3}/_{8}$" x $^{3}/_{8}$" groove
2	Side panels	$^{3}/_{4}$ x $12^{5}/_{8}$ x $12^{5}/_{8}$	Maple	$^{1}/_{2}$" x $^{3}/_{8}$" rabbet on edges; rests in $^{3}/_{8}$" x $^{3}/_{8}$" groove
1	Back panel	$^{3}/_{4}$ x $12^{5}/_{8}$ x $20^{5}/_{8}$	Maple	$^{1}/_{2}$" x $^{3}/_{8}$" rabbet on edges; rests in $^{3}/_{8}$" x $^{3}/_{8}$" groove

DOORS

No.	Item	Dimensions T W L	Material	Comments
4	Stiles	$^{1}/_{2}$ x $1^{1}/_{2}$ x $12^{1}/_{2}$	Maple	
4	Rails	$^{1}/_{2}$ x $1^{3}/_{4}$ x $9^{1}/_{2}$	Maple	1" TBE
2	Panels	$^{1}/_{4}$ x $8^{1}/_{4}$ x $9^{3}/_{4}$	Ply	in $^{1}/_{4}$" x $^{3}/_{8}$" rabbet on back of door
8	Slats	$^{1}/_{8}$ x 1 x $7^{1}/_{2}$	Maple	applied to panel

KEY: TBE = tenon on both ends.

asian bedside table millimeters

TOP

No.	Item	Dimensions T W L	Material	Comments
2	Top stiles	45 x 45 x 762	Maple	10mm x 10mm groove on inside edge
2	Top rails	45 x 45 x 457	Maple	25mm TBE, 10mm x 10mm groove on inside edge
1	Panel	19 x 419 x 521	Maple	in 10mm x 10mm groove; 13mm x 10mm rabbet, all sides

BASE

No.	Item	Dimensions T W L	Material	Comments
4	Legs	45 x 45 x 584	Maple	10mm x 10mm groove for side & back panels
4	Rails for sides	25 x 38 x 356	Maple	25mm TBE, 10mm x 10mm groove for side panels
3	Rails frt & bk	25 x 38 x 559	Maple	25mm TBE, 10mm x10mm groove for back panel
1	Front bottom rail	51 x 38 x 559	Maple	25mm TBE
2	Top & bot panels	19 x 324 x 527	Maple	13mm x 10mm rabbet on edges; rests in 10mm x 10mm groove
2	Side panels	19 x 321 x 321	Maple	13mm x 10mm rabbet on edges; rests in 10mm x 10mm groove
1	Back panel	19 x 321 x 524	Maple	13mm x 10mm rabbet on edges; rests in 10mm x 10mm groove

DOORS

No.	Item	Dimensions T W L	Material	Comments
4	Stiles	13 x 38 x 318	Maple	
4	Rails	13 x 45 x 242	Maple	25mm TBE
2	Panels	6 x 209 x 248	Ply	in 6mm x 10mm rabbet on back of door
8	Slats	3 x 25 x 191	Maple	applied to panel

KEY: TBE = tenon on both ends.

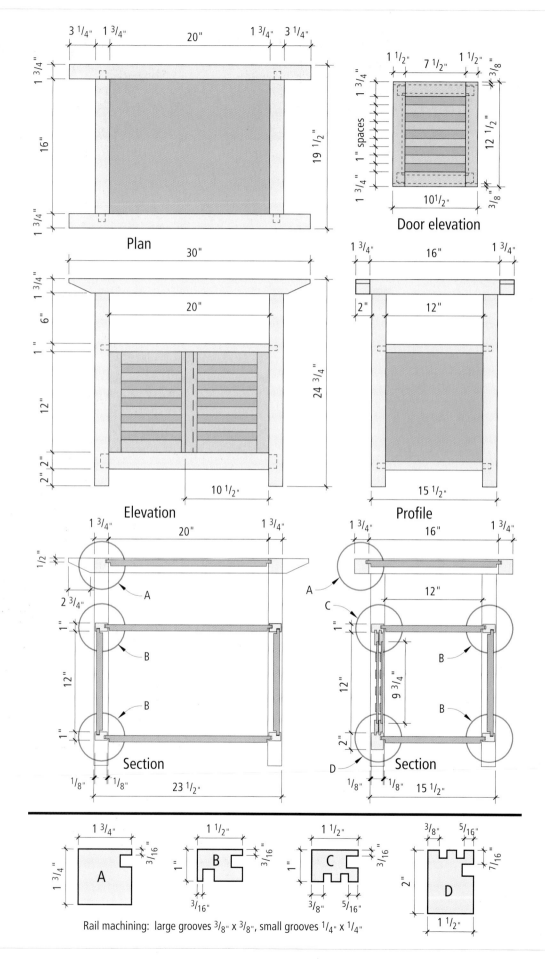

3 1/4" 1 3/4" 20" 1 3/4" 3 1/4"

1 3/4"

16"

19 1/2"

1 3/4"

Plan

1 1/2" 7 1/2" 1 1/2"

1 3/4"

3/8"

1" spaces

1 3/4"

12 1/2"

10 1/2"

3/8"

Door elevation

30"

1 3/4"

6"

1"

20"

24 3/4"

12"

2" 2"

10 1/2"

Elevation

1 3/4" 16" 1 3/4"

2"

12"

15 1/2"

Profile

1 3/4" 20" 1 3/4"

1/2"

A

2 3/4"

1"

B

12"

B

1"

Section

1/8" 1/8" 23 1/2"

1 3/4" 16" 1 3/4"

A

12"

C

1"

B

12"

9 3/4"

B

2"

D

Section

1/8" 1/8" 15 1/2"

1 3/4"

1 3/4"

3/16"

A

1 1/2"

1"

B

3/16"

3/16"

1 1/2"

1"

C

3/16"

3/8" 5/16"

3/8" 5/16"

3/8" 5/16"

2"

D

7/16"

1 1/2"

Rail machining: large grooves 3/8" x 3/8", small grooves 1/4" x 1/4"

Two Grooves for Every Rail

There are lots of grooves on the rails and in the legs. One way to cut them all is by using a $\frac{3}{8}$" straight bit and a router table setup. However, I like to see what's going on when I cut grooves like these, so I used an aftermarket edge guide on my router. I prefer the Micro Fence for work such as this because it allows me to sneak right up on the perfect measurement with its microadjustable knob. Other edge guides are capable of the job, however.

Set your $\frac{3}{8}$" straight bit so it will make a $\frac{3}{8}$"-deep cut, and set your fence so the bit is $\frac{3}{16}$" from the fence. Now, working from the outside edges of the rails, cut the $\frac{3}{8}$" × $\frac{3}{8}$" grooves on all the rails that hold the panels, except for the groove in the bottom front rail that holds the bottom panel. To cut that groove, set the distance between the fence and bit to $\frac{7}{16}$" and fire away. See the drawings on page 68 for more detail.

Now cut the grooves in the legs for the panels. Set your bit so it's $\frac{5}{16}$" from the fence and essentially connect the mortises.

Now it's time to cut the two grooves in the two front rails that the doors ride in. Chuck a $\frac{1}{4}$" straight bit in your router and cut the grooves in the top and bottom rails.

To make the panels fit in their grooves, cut a $\frac{3}{8}$"-deep × $\frac{1}{2}$"-long rabbet on the underside of all the panels. You're going to have to notch the corners of each panel to fit around the legs. Cut the notches using a backsaw.

Finish sand all the parts for the case and get ready for assembly. Check the fit of the doors in the grooves. A couple passes with a shoulder plane on the tongues made my doors slide smoothly. Once everything fits, glue the side assemblies up. Put glue in the mortises, but not in the grooves. You'll want to finish everything before final assembly, so set the side assemblies and the rest of the parts aside for later.

The Top: Still More Grooves

The top is made much the same as the sides. First cut the $\frac{1}{2}$"-thick × 1"-long

On the door slats, I cheated. I didn't feel like mortising the really thin stock into the stiles. To ensure that your spacing is correct, use a couple of 1"-wide spacers to place your slats. A piece of tape on mine shimmed the spacers a bit to ensure the slats were equally spaced.

Again, when cutting the grooves you want to move the router in the direction opposite the rotation of the cutterhead. In this instance, it means moving the router from left to right.

QUICK TIPS: STRATEGIES FOR RIDDING YOUR JOINTS OF GAPS

When you do a lot of mortise-and-tenon work, one of the most frustrating aspects of the joint is trying to get a seamless fit. Here are a few tricks to ensure fewer gaps.

1. Pay attention to the edge of the board that the mortise is in. If you sand or plane this surface before assembly, chances are you're going to change the angle of the edge, which will give you a gap when you assemble the joint. Before I cut a mortise in an edge I run it over my jointer slowly to remove any saw marks. After the joint is glued and assembled, I clean up the jointer marks with 120-grit sandpaper.

2. On highly visible joints I put the tenoned piece in my vise and work on it with a chisel. Pare away at the shoulder area around and up to the tenon — but stay away from the edge. You only need to remove about $1/32$" of material.

3. Make your mortises $1/16$" deeper than your tenons are long. This stops your tenons from bottoming out in the mortises and gives any excess glue a place to collect.

Here's where it all comes together. You can see the grooves for the panels in the rails, legs and mitered tenons.

My large shoulder plane is probably one of the most useful tools in my shop. It trims tenons and deepens rabbets better than anything else out there. The original Record 073 (now out of production) sells used for several hundred dollars. I bought my Lie-Nielsen version for $225. Pricey? Yes, but well worth it. When you trim the tongues on the doors, make sure you have something backing up your cut or you will blow out the end grain.

BOOKSHELF

If you're interested in Asian furniture, tools and construction methods, I recommend the following books available from The Japan Woodworker, 800-537-7820:

The Complete Japanese Joinery by Hideo Sato, item # 03.241, $29.95

The Art of Japanese Joinery by Kiyosi Seike, item # 03.009, $16.95

Traditional Japanese Furniture by Kazuko Koizumi, item # 03.195, $85

Japanese Woodworking Tools: Their Spirit, Tradition and Use by Toshio Odate, item # 03.250.25, $24.95

tenons on the ends of the rails. Cut the mortises to match in the stiles. Get out your router and your fence again, chuck the $^3/_8$" straight bit in there and set the distance between the bit and the fence to $^3/_{16}$". This will make the top recess into the frame. Set the depth of cut to $^3/_8$" and cut the grooves in the rails and the stiles.

Cut the detail on the ends of the stiles as shown in the drawings on page 68. I cut it using my band saw, and cleaned up the bevel using a plane. Finally, cut a $^3/_8$"-deep × $^1/_2$"-long rabbet on the bottom side of your panel. Finish sand all the parts and glue up the top frame.

Finish and Fit

Before finishing, apply masking tape to all the tenons and plug the mortises with packing peanuts. Apply three coats of a clear finish, such as clear shellac or lacquer, and sand between each coat. When the finish has fully cured, assemble the case. Apply glue in the mortises, slide the doors in place and clamp it up. Check the case for square across the height and depth. When the glue is dry, attach the top using desktop fasteners, sometimes called figure-8 fasteners. With a $^3/_4$" Forstner bit chucked into your hand drill, cut a recess for the fastener in the top of each leg. Screw the fasteners to

the legs. Then screw the case to the underside of the top.

Whenever I finish a project such as this, I can't help but look askance at the tiny imperfections (unnoticeable to most people) that come from handwork. But then I try to remember another Zen saying from Ts'ai Ken T'An that should comfort all woodworkers: "Water which is too pure has no fish."

Supplies

Rockler • 800-279-4441, or www.rockler.com
Desk top fasteners - # 21650

Micro Fence • 800-480-6427, or www.microfence.com

all-in-one cabinet
for the small shop

This shop cabinet squeezes 13 cubic feet of tool storage into less than 3 square feet of floor space.

If you're like most woodworkers, your shop is packed to the gills with tools, tooling and accessories. Storing power tools on open shelves is no good; dust gets into the windings and shortens the life of the motors. You need an enclosed cabinet, and you need one that takes up less floor space than a band saw. This cabinet has a place to store routers, all the bits a woodworker could need and other accessories such as edge guides, bases and template guides. There's also room for tools such as jigsaws, sanders, biscuit joiners and even a portable planer.

Build the Case

Before cutting the plywood, it would be helpful to check out the optimization diagram on our Web site, www.popwood.com, which shows you how to lay out the parts on two sheets of plywood. After the parts are cut to size, cut $\frac{1}{2}$" × $\frac{3}{4}$" rabbets on the ends of the sides to hold the top and bottom pieces. Unless your shop has high ceilings, you'll need to cut the rabbets with a plunge router, straight bit and an edge guide. First set the router for the finished depth using your turret depth stop. Then raise the bit halfway and make a pass that defines the shoulder of the rabbet. Climb cut (which is basically routing in reverse, moving the router backwards) the waste out to the edge of the board. Finally, plunge to the full depth of your rabbet and repeat the above procedure.

The next step is to cut the ¼" × ¾" dadoes in the sides. Mark the location of the dado and make a simple jig to rout it. The jig uses a bearing-on-top straight bit to guide against the edges of the jig. To make the jig, take the fixed shelf and place two strips of plywood against it on a flat surface. Place all of this on top of two cross pieces on either end of the strips and glue and nail them in place. Leave a little room (about ½") across the length of the dado cut to adjust the jig. Clamp the jig on the marked lines and rout the dado in two passes. Finish machining the sides by cutting the ½" × ¼" rabbet for the back on the back edge of both sides, top and bottom. If the cabinet won't be attached to the wall, use a thicker back for stability. Check the top, bottom and fixed shelf for a good fit, then glue and nail or screw the cabinet together. Fit the back and set it aside. Place the case on a flat work surface and add iron-on edging. Finish the case by gluing and nailing the hanging rail into the top of the case, flush with the rabbet in the back.

Build the Base

Next build the adjustable base. Back when I made custom cabinetry, we often added an adjustable-height base to cabinets like this one to compensate for uneven floors or walls. The base is a simple plywood rectangle with adjustable feet attached to the inside corners, and drilled holes in the case above the feet. This allows you to adjust the base with a screwdriver while the cabinet is in place.

The base itself is a simple mitered frame, with biscuits added at the

Here's the simple jig used to rout the dadoes. It uses a bearing-on-top straight bit to guide against the edges of the jig. Clamp the jig right on the marked lines and rout the dado.

Use screws and glue to attach the levelers to the inside corners of the base frame. The top of the block — the end opposite the foot — should be flush with the top edge of the base frame.

miters. Cut the miters, then glue and clamp the base together. Make sure the base is square by measuring across the corners.

While the glue dries, cut out the blocks that hold the adjustable feet. They're 1½" × 1½" × 3¼" blocks. Drill a centered ⁷⁄₁₆" hole through the length of the block for a T-nut. Drill holes at

right angles to one another in the block that will be used to screw the blocks to the base. Hammer in the T-nuts. With the feet threaded into the blocks the entire assembly is about 4" long, and should flush up with the top and bottom of the base frame.

Now it's time to attach the base. Cut out four ¾" × ¾" cleats that fit between

With the case on its back, take two hand screws and attach them to the back lip of the case, ¼" in from the back. This provides a little offset for the moulding on your walls. If you have larger base moulding, make the base a little taller or less deep to accommodate the larger moulding. Place the base up against the case bottom. Center it on the bottom and temporarily screw it into place with four 1¼" screws.

Take out all the feet and use a pencil to mark the location of the top of the leveler hole. Remove the base and drill ½" holes into the case bottom.

the levelers, and drill mounting holes in the cleats for attaching the case bottom. Screw them in place about ¹/₃₂" down from the top edge of the base. Make sure to position the base on the bottom. Temporarily screw the base in place with four 1¼" screws. Take out the feet and use a pencil to mark the location of the top of the leveler hole. Drill the holes using a piece of scrap to back up the hole or you'll tear out the veneer on the inside of the case bottom. When you reattach the base you'll be able to adjust the levelers using a screwdriver.

all-in-one cabinet for the small shop **inches**

No.	Item	Dimensions T W L	Material
2	Sides	¾ x 16 x 68	Birch ply
2	Top and bottom	¾ x 16 x 23½	Birch ply
1	Fixed shelf	¾ x 15¾ x 23	Birch ply
4	Shelves	¾ x 15½ x 22½	Birch ply
1	Back	¼ x 23½ x 67½	Birch ply
4	Doors*	¾ x 12 x 29¼	Birch ply
2	Base front and back	¾ x 4 x 23½	Birch ply
2	Base sides	¾ x 4 x 14	Birch ply
1	Cleat for base	¾ x ¾ x 96	Solid wood
4	Leveler blocks	1½ x 1½ x 3¼	Solid wood
1	Support cleat	¾ x 3 x 23½	Birch ply
1	Drawer front*	¾ x 9⅜ x 24	Birch ply
2	Drawer sides	½ x 8 x 15½	Baltic birch
2	Drawer front and back	½ x 8 x 21	Baltic birch
1	Drawer bottom	¼ x 15 x 21	Baltic birch
2	Drawer rails	½ x 1 x 20½	Baltic birch
1	Drawer insert slider	¾ x 14½ x 12	Birch ply
1	Drawer lid	½ x 12½ x 21½	Baltic birch
1	Lid back rail	½ x 3 x 21½	Baltic birch

* Finished size with bullnose edging attached

all-in-one cabinet for the small shop **millimeters**

No.	Item	Dimensions T W L	Material
2	Sides	19 x 406 x 1727	Birch ply
2	Top and bottom	19 x 406 x 597	Birch ply
1	Fixed shelf	19 x 400 x 584	Birch ply
4	Shelves	19 x 394 x 572	Birch ply
1	Back	6 x 597 x 1715	Birch ply
4	Doors*	19 x 305 x 743	Birch ply
2	Base front and back	19 x 102 x 597	Birch ply
2	Base sides	19 x 102 x 356	Birch ply
1	Cleat for base	19 x 19 x 2438	Solid wood
4	Leveler blocks	38 x 38 x 82	Solid wood
1	Support cleat	19 x 76 x 597	Birch ply
1	Drawer front*	19 x 239 x 610	Birch ply
2	Drawer sides	13 x 203 x 394	Baltic birch
2	Drawer front and back	13 x 203 x 533	Baltic birch
1	Drawer bottom	6 x 381 x 533	Baltic birch
2	Drawer rails	13 x 25 x 521	Baltic birch
1	Drawer insert slider	19 x 369 x 305	Birch ply
1	Drawer lid	13 x 318 x 546	Baltic birch
1	Lid back rail	13 x 76 x 546	Baltic birch

* Finished size with bullnose edging attached

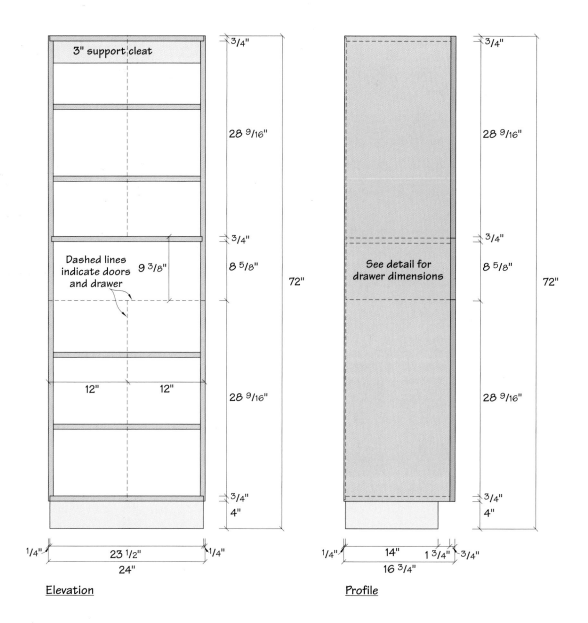

3" support cleat

3/4"

28 9/16"

3/4"

Dashed lines
indicate doors
and drawer

9 3/8"

8 5/8"

72"

12"   12"

28 9/16"

3/4"
4"

1/4"   23 1/2"   1/4"
24"

Elevation

3/4"

28 9/16"

3/4"

See detail for
drawer dimensions

8 5/8"

72"

28 9/16"

3/4"
4"

1/4"   14"   1 3/4"   3/4"
16 3/4"

Profile

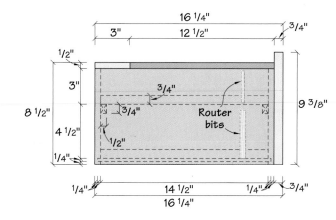

16 1/4"

3"   12 1/2"   3/4"

1/2"

3"

8 1/2"

3/4"

3/4"

Router
bits

9 3/8"

4 1/2"

1/2"

1/4"

1/4"   14 1/2"   1/4"   3/4"
16 1/4"

Profile of Drawer

Build the Doors

The doors are plywood slabs with mitered moulding nailed to the edges. The moulding is a $^{3}/_{16}$" × $^{13}/_{16}$" solid wood edge with a bullnose routed on the front. The bullnose is referred to as a cockbead, which is a common detail on period furniture from the 18th and 19th centuries, and is an easy way to dress up a door or drawer front.

After the edging has been applied, it's impossible to sand into the corners, so begin making the doors by finish sanding the fronts of the doors and drawers. Next attach the moulding. Apply two opposite pieces, then fit and attach the last two pieces.

Use a sharp pencil to mark the location of the miter cuts. Place the piece on the miter saw and cut to the line. You don't always get the cut right the first time. Make your cut a little long and nibble away at the miter until you get a snug fit, then glue and nail the edges in place. I used Accuset's micropinner to attach the mouldings; the 23-gauge pins don't split the edge, and they leave a hole about the size of a period on this page. Putty the holes if you like. Rout off any overhang on the back side with a router and straight bit. Finish sand the backs.

Now you're ready to hang the doors. The cups for European cabinet hinges are usually 35mm or close to 1$^{3}/_{8}$".

Using the instructions that came with the hinges, derive a drilling location for the hinge cup. I always drill hinge cups about 3" or 4" in from the top and bottom of the door. This leaves enough room to adjust the hinge when it is mounted.

First, drill the hinge cup holes. Set your drill press to drill the holes a little deeper than the cup. Then transfer the layout holes to the door on the cabinet. Attach the mounting plate and screw the hinges in place. European hinges can be adjusted in three different ways: in-out, up-down and left-right. When the cabinet is level and plumb, adjust the hinges to make the doors even.

After cutting the stock according to the diagram on page 76, take a piece and cut a miter on one end. Be sure to make the first cut with the bullnose up. This isn't important for the first two edges, but it's very important for the last two. Use a piece of scrap with a miter cut on both ends to test the fit of the miters.

When fitting the second set of edges, start by cutting the miter on one end. Flip the edge over and place what will be the bottom edge of the miter into the miter on the right. Gently press the flat edge against the other miter. Mark the location of the miter and make the cut.

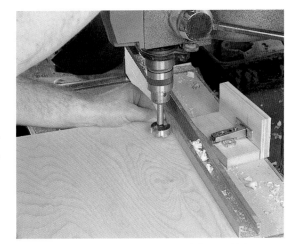

Drill the holes for the hinge cups on your drill press. Make a test piece using a hinge and mounting plate to test your setup.

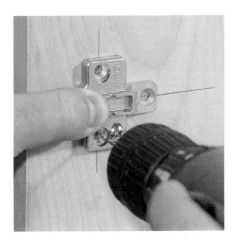

Lay the plate on the marks and drill pilot holes into the cabinet.

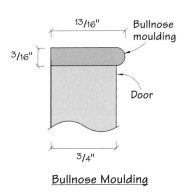

13/16"
Bullnose moulding

3/16"

Door

3/4"

Bullnose Moulding

Build the Router Bit Drawer

The drawer requires standard construction. Cut $\frac{1}{4}" \times \frac{1}{2}"$ rabbets on the ends of the sides. Cut a $\frac{1}{4}" \times \frac{1}{4}"$ groove in the bottom inside edges of all the parts to hold the bottom. Glue and nail the drawer together with the bottom set into the groove.

After the glue is dry, take apart the commercial drawer slides, scribe a line on the sides and attach the small part of the slide to the drawer box. Make sure it's flush to the front of the drawer box. Measure from the mounting line and add $\frac{3}{4}"$ to that for the lid, hinges and gap. Measure that distance down from the inside, underneath the fixed shelf. Mark the location and mount the slide. The slides have two different mounting holes. The drawer has slots that allow up and down adjustment, and the cabinet parts have slots that allow forward/backward adjustment. Insert the drawer into the slides on the cabinet.

Before mounting the front on the drawer box, nail two finish nails through the front of the drawer box until they just protrude from the outside. Place the front against the drawer box and space it so the gaps on the top and bottom are equal. Push the front against the nails in the drawer box and gently push out the drawer. Drill some clearance holes and attach the front.

Now nail on the drawer lid's back rail and attach the lid with two hinges. Drill a 1" hole in the lid so you can lift it easily. Cut out, drill and attach the two router storage inserts.

Finish up the project by drilling a series of 7mm holes for the shelf pins. Make a template from scrap for this. Lee Valley sells metal sleeves for the shelf pins, but I deemed them unnecessary. You could probably get away with using a $\frac{1}{4}"$ bit to make these holes, but the pins will fit a little sloppily. Attach the back with #6 $\times \frac{1}{2}"$ flathead screws. Check the fit of all the doors, drawer and shelves, then disassemble all the loose parts for sanding. Apply three coats of clear finish and reassemble all the parts.

After attaching the slide to the drawer, mark the location of the corresponding slide on the cabinet side. Use a framing square to run a line back from this mark, and mount the slide $\frac{1}{16}"$ back from the front of the cabinet.

Position the drawer front and place a couple of clamps on the drawer box to hold it in place. Drill countersunk clearance holes into the drawer box and attach the front with 1" screws.

Supplies

Lee Valley • 800-871-8158, or www.leevalley.com

4 - 107° Full overlay hinges - #00B10.01
1 - 14" Full ext. drawer slides - #02K10.14
4 - 4" Swivel levelers - #01S06.04
4 - $\frac{3}{8}"$-16 T-nuts (10 pc.) - #00N22.24
5 - 4" Wire pulls - #01W78.04
1 - Coat hook - #00W80.01
24 - Shelf pins (50pc.) - #94Z03.02
1 - 25' Maple edge banding - #41A05.01
2 - 25mm x 15mm hinges - #00D30.08
8 - #1 $\times \frac{3}{8}"$ screws (10pc.) - #91Z01.02

This is offered by Lee Valley as a package. Ask for item #05D1510

Note: The screws supplied with the hinges use a #1 drive. You'll need a small #1 square drive bit.

Drill the ½" and ¼" holes. Nail in a couple of rails on the inside of the drawer and simply drop the panels in place. The panel for ½"-shank bits is drilled all the way through and the panel for ¼"-shank bits is drilled down ⅝".

Use a stop collar on your drill bit when drilling holes for the shelf pins. I made this drilling jig from shop scrap.

traditional
entertainment center

Don't be intimidated by the size of this case;
the joinery is simple yet rock solid.

I chuckle to myself every time I build one of these cabinets for a customer. A Shaker entertainment center — now that's an oxymoron. But everybody loves Shaker and everyone needs an entertainment center these days. So who am I to argue?

As cabinet construction goes, this is about as basic as it gets, but it still offers old-world joinery, styling and strength. The entire piece is solid lumber, with a face-frame front and a shiplapped back. The raised-panel doors are held together with mortise-and-tenon joinery, and the crown moulding is made with simple cuts on the table saw and jointer.

I start construction on face-frame cabinets by making the face frame first. All the other pieces will be sized to fit the frame, so it makes sense to begin there. Also, the width of the face frame's stiles are $1/16$" wider than shown in the drawing. This allows you to trim them flush to the case after assembly.

There are a number of ways to fasten a face frame together, but when I'm making a piece of furniture that has the potential to be moved every so often I prefer the strongest joint I can think of — mortise and tenon. That's because if it's moving, it's racking. While a strong back helps keep the cabinet from racking, the face frame does most of the work. In addition, if the piece is a reproduction, like the one here, it's appropriate to use a mortise-and-tenon frame.

Cut the tenons on the ends of the rails first, then use those tenons to lay out the mortises on the stiles. Set up your table saw to cut the $3/8$" × 1"-long tenons, centered on both ends of the top and bottom rails. Then set up your mortiser to cut the mating mortises, setting your depth to $1^1/16$" to avoid having the tenon bottom out in the mortise.

Once the mortises and tenons are cut, assemble the frame by squeezing glue into the mortises. Don't overdo it; glue can keep the tenon from seating properly in the mortise. After the glue is dry, pin the joints using $\frac{3}{8}$"-square stock.

Three-Panel Doors

Since I'm already set up for making mortise-and-tenon joints, I make the doors next. The doors are basic frame-and-panel construction using raised panels with an 8° bevel on the front face. Determine the size of the doors by making them exactly the size of the opening in the face frame. We'll trim them to fit later.

Before cutting the joints for the doors I make the groove in the rails and stiles for the raised panels. These grooves are $\frac{3}{8}$" × $\frac{3}{8}$" and are centered on the inside edge of each piece, with both edges of the center rails receiving a groove. After the grooves are run, start making the tenons on each end of the rails. Make the tenons and mortises the same size as you used for the face frame. Because the panel groove was run through the ends of each stile, the tenons on the top and bottom rails need to be haunched — the tenon shoulder is wider to fill the notch left by the groove.

Next mark the locations for the mortises at the locations shown in the diagrams, and cut the mortises in the stiles.

The panels themselves are cut to size, allowing $\frac{1}{2}$" extra in both height and width to fit into the grooves in the door frame. With the panels sized, set your table saw blade to an 8° angle. Then set the rip fence to bevel the faces of the panels. Set the distance between the fence and blade so the bevel is about $\frac{3}{8}$"-thick, $\frac{1}{4}$" in from each edge.

When the door pieces are ready, assemble the doors. Be careful not to use too much glue on the joints. Clamp up the doors and determine if the doors are square by measuring corner to corner. The distance should be the same in both directions. If not, adjust the

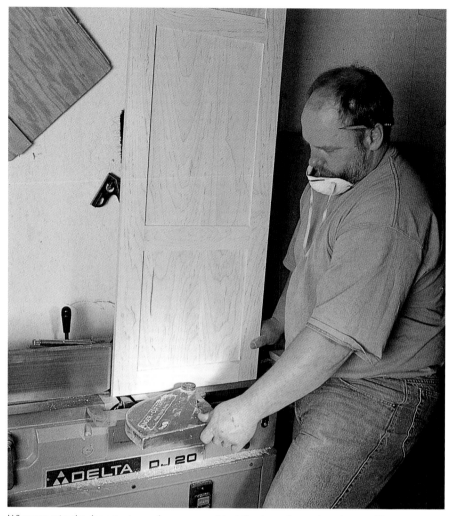

When you trim the doors to size, make sure you support the door adequately and start with the top and bottom edges. That way any tear-out on the end grain will be removed when you run the long-grain edges over the jointer.

After the face frame is glued to the cabinet, walk around the case with a flush-cutting bit in your router to trim the frame flush to the cabinet. A little sanding and you're ready to move on.

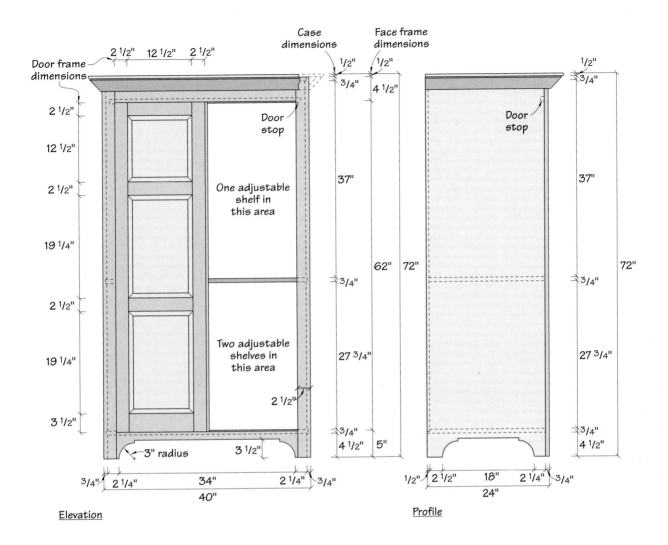

Elevation

Profile

No.	Item	Dimensions T W L	Material
2	Face frame stiles	$\frac{3}{4} \times 2\frac{9}{16} \times 71\frac{1}{2}$	Maple
1	Face frame top rail*	$\frac{3}{4} \times 4\frac{1}{2} \times 37$	Maple
1	Face frame bottom rail*	$\frac{3}{4} \times 5 \times 37$	Maple
3	Door stiles	$\frac{3}{4} \times 2\frac{1}{2} \times 62$	Maple
1	Door stile	$\frac{3}{4} \times 3 \times 62$	Maple
6	Door rails*	$\frac{3}{4} \times 3\frac{1}{2} \times 14\frac{1}{2}$	Maple
2	Door bottom rails	$\frac{3}{4} \times 3\frac{1}{2} \times 14\frac{1}{2}$	Maple
2	Door panels	$\frac{5}{8} \times 13 \times 13$	Maple
4	Door panels	$\frac{5}{8} \times 13 \times 19\frac{3}{4}$	Maple
2	Cabinet sides	$\frac{3}{4} \times 23\frac{1}{4} \times 71\frac{1}{2}$	Maple
3	Fixed shelves	$\frac{3}{4} \times 22\frac{3}{4} \times 39$	Maple
3	Adjustable shelves	$\frac{3}{4} \times 22\frac{1}{4} \times 38\frac{1}{4}$	Maple
1	Back	$\frac{1}{2} \times 39\frac{1}{2} \times 71\frac{1}{2}$	Maple
1	Door stop	$\frac{3}{4} \times \frac{7}{8} \times 37$	Maple
1	Crown moulding	$\frac{3}{4} \times 3\frac{3}{4} \times 96$	Maple
1	Crown cap	$\frac{1}{2} \times 3\frac{1}{8} \times 96$	Maple
6	Hinges, Lee Valley #00H52.03, 800-871-8158 or www.leevalley.com		

Measurement includes a 1"-long tenon on both ends

No.	Item	Dimensions T W L	Material
2	Face frame stiles	19 x 65 x 1816	Maple
1	Face frame top rail*	19 x 115 x 940	Maple
1	Face frame bottom rail*	19 x 127 x 940	Maple
3	Door stiles	19 x 64 x 1575	Maple
1	Door stile	19 x 76 x 1575	Maple
6	Door rails*	19 x 89 x 369	Maple
2	Door bottom rails	19 x 89 x 369	Maple
2	Door panels	16 x 330 x 330	Maple
4	Door panels	16 x 330 x 502	Maple
2	Cabinet sides	19 x 590 x 1816	Maple
3	Fixed shelves	19 x 579 x 991	Maple
3	Adjustable shelves	19 x 565 x 971	Maple
1	Back	13 x 1004 x 1816	Maple
1	Door stop	19 x 22 x 940	Maple
1	Crown moulding	19 x 95 x 2438	Maple
1	Crown cap	13 x 79 x 2438	Maple
6	Hinges, Lee Valley #00H52.03, 800-871-8158 or www.leevalley.com		

Measurement includes a 25mm-long tenon on both ends

traditional entertainment center **inches**

traditional entertainment center **millimeters**

door by tightening a clamp diagonally across the longer length. When everything is square, tighten the clamps, set the doors aside and let the glue cure.

When the doors are ready, use your saw to cut a $\frac{3}{8}$" × $\frac{1}{2}$" rabbet on the two interior edges, forming a shiplap joint to keep the dust out. Then head to the jointer and trim them to size, allowing a $\frac{1}{16}$" gap all the way around the doors. When fitting the doors, run the top and bottom of them over the jointer first, as the end grain on the ends of the stiles may tear out. By running the long-grain edges last you should be able to clean up any tear-out on the stiles.

With the doors fit, mount the doors in the face frame. I used $2\frac{1}{2}$" non-mortise butt hinges. They look good, are easy to attach and are adjustable. When the doors are attached, take them off again to make it easier to glue up the cabinet.

Cabinet: Dadoes and Nails

You're now ready to make the cabinet itself. All the cabinet pieces are made of solid lumber and therefore reproduction quality. The center shelf, top and bottom are fit into $\frac{1}{4}$"-deep × $\frac{3}{4}$"-wide dadoes in the sides. Use the diagrams to locate the dadoes. The sides of the cabinet have $\frac{3}{8}$" × $\frac{1}{2}$" rabbets run on the inside edges for the back. Cut the dadoes, then glue and nail the top, bottom and center shelf between the sides.

After assembling the case, lay it on its back and glue and clamp the face frame to the cabinet. Check for square, and make sure the overhang on the sides is even. When the glue is dry, simply remove the clamps and use a flush-cutting router bit to trim the face frame flush to the sides.

I used a $\frac{1}{2}$" hardwood beaded shiplap back for this piece. The number of back slats is up to you. They can be random widths, or they can all be the same. I cut a $\frac{1}{4}$" × $\frac{1}{2}$" rabbet on the slat sides, then add a $\frac{1}{4}$" bead on one edge using a beading bit in my router table. Don't attach the back yet; doing so only makes finishing more difficult. Set the pieces aside for now.

To bevel the crown pieces, first bevel cut one edge with the table saw blade set at 45°. Then move to your jointer — also set at 45° — and put a $\frac{1}{4}$" flat at a right angle to your first bevel.

Cut the second bevel. By cutting the return bevel on the first edge you've provided a bearing surface for the rip fence, rather than let the bevel slip under the fence, making a bad cut.

One last pass on the jointer and you're ready to hang the crown.

Shaker furniture is known for its lack of ornamentation, but the Shakers still had a sense of style. Style for this cabinet requires a crown moulding. Cut the moulding pieces to the sizes given in the Materials List. Set your table saw blade to a 45° angle and bevel one long edge of the moulding piece. Then adjust the fence on your jointer to 45° and run the sharp bevel edge of the moulding over it leaving $\frac{1}{4}$" flat on the moulding's edge. Repeat the entire process on the opposite edge.

Fit and cut the crown pieces to

length, then glue and nail them to the case. On the side pieces I only glue the first 8" of the moulding and attach the back end with a screw through a slotted hole in the case. This allows the sides of the case to move during humidity changes without tearing the crown moulding off. I use small triangular glue blocks behind the crown moulding to support the crown. Next cut the $\frac{1}{2}$" cap pieces to length, mitering them to overhang the crown by $\frac{1}{4}$", then attach them to the case as well.

To make sure the crown moulding is flush to the top of the cabinet, I temporarily screw two scrap strips to the top of the cabinet while I align the front piece. When the front piece is attached, it's fairly easy to carry the height orientation to the sides. Then simply remove the strips.

A Simple Base

You're almost done. To give the case a base — and to make it sit on an uneven floor without rocking — I used a jigsaw to cut out a pattern on the bottom of the face frame and the sides of the piece, essentially leaving legs. Drill the holes for the shelf pins. Then cut slots for ventilation in the back, and holes through the shelves to pass wires.

The next to last step was finishing. I used a coat of dark oak stain over the entire piece, then applied three coats of semigloss spray lacquer.

All that's left is the hardware. You can use whatever you find attractive. I used a couple of turned pulls and added a stop rail behind the doors, at the top of the cabinet. After installing a couple of bullet catches, I was ready to deliver it to the customer. Of course it will take them another two days to get all the equipment hooked up and arranged the way they want, but that's another project.

The last step to installing the crown is to attach the cap to the crown and cabinet. Notice the glue blocks behind the crown moulding support the crown and add stability.

pennsylvania **spice box**

Build this 18th century spice box with a
raised-panel or original-style marquetry door.

The idea of trying marquetry came to me after seeing a picture of a particularly fine specimen in a book called *Pennsylvania Spice Boxes* by Lee Ellen Griffith. Feeling much more comfortable with tools that plug in, however, I studied the picture of a highly inlaid spice box for some time, trying to figure out how to adapt modern power tools to a very hand tool driven skill. It took me a while, but I finally gave it a try — fully expecting to fall on my face. So that my time wouldn't be a total loss if I messed up, I first built the spice box with a raised-panel door. After that, I tried the marquetry door. I figured if all went well, great. If not, I'd still have a nice spice box. Turns out, I got both.

Somewhat Complex Casework

The construction for this box itself is actually more complicated than you'd expect from such a little thing. The sides are dovetailed to the case top, while the bottom is fit into dadoes cut in the sides. The back rests in a rabbet, and the center dividers for the drawers are joined with dadoes to one another and to the case.

Start construction by gluing up panels (unless you have some nice wide boards) and cutting the sides, bottom, top and dividers to the sizes given. Most of the joinery is done with stopped dadoes. Though you can make through-dadoes with a table saw, stopped dadoes are easier to make with a router. I used a trim router to form the $\frac{1}{4}$"-wide dadoes in the sides for the drawer partitions. Cut each dado $\frac{7}{16}$" deep and $7\frac{1}{8}$" long, starting from the back edge of each side. Locate the dadoes by using the diagrams on page 89. And remember, you're making right- and left-handed pieces.

While you have a $\frac{1}{4}$" bit set up in a router, run the $\frac{1}{8}$"-deep dadoes in the drawer dividers to form the interlocking divider assembly. You might be tempted to nail the interior assembly together now, but wait until you can dry fit it with the rest of the case assembled.

Next, change to a $\frac{3}{4}$"-diameter pattern-cutting bit and cut the dadoes in the sides for the bottom, using a straightedge as a guide. A smaller diameter bit will do, just make a couple of passes to achieve the final width.

Then use the same setup to form the rabbets on the sides for the back boards. The bottom dado is $\frac{3}{8}$" deep and it starts 2" up from the bottom. The back rabbet is $\frac{5}{8}$" × $\frac{7}{16}$" and runs the full length of the side.

The door fits onto the case by cutting a stopped rabbet on the left side piece and notching out the right side. Make the $\frac{1}{4}$" × $\frac{3}{4}$" stopped rabbet using a router, starting at the top edge of the lower dado and stopping $1\frac{1}{2}$" down from the top edge of the side. Square out the rabbet using a sharp chisel and mallet. To notch the right side I used my table saw, again starting at the top edge of the lower dado and stopping 1½" down from the top edge of the side.

The next step is to cut the through-dovetails to mate the top to the sides. Use whatever dovetailing method you prefer. I cut mine by hand to give the piece an authentic period appearance.

The last step before assembly is to cut away the lower part of each side up to the previously cut dado, leaving "feet" on either side. This cutaway allows you to attach the bottom (resting in the exposed dado, which now becomes essentially a rabbet) to the sides using cut nails, and allows the lower moulding to appear open below the cabinet, but makes attaching the moulding simple and strong. Use the moulding patterns to locate the cutaways, holding the top edge at the bottom of the lower dadoes.

After some interior sanding, round over the leading edges of the drawer partitions a fair amount to give the interior a more finished appearance. You're now ready to assemble the case. Start with the dovetails, then slip the

TIPS ON WOOD PUTTY

One of the tricky parts about using wood putty to hide nail holes is matching the wood's color. Store-bought putty comes in an array of colors, but may not dry the same color as it appears when wet. In addition, if you match the putty to the color of the wood prior to finishing the piece, you may find that the putty doesn't change in color when the finish is applied.

To avoid this problem, apply some finish to a scrap piece, then match your purchased putty to the sample. This may take a couple of tries, but it's well worth the effort. Some manufactured putties indicate that they will take a stain. This may be true, but I still recommend making a test piece.

Another method would be to make your own putty using sanding dust from the wood you are using and white or yellow wood glue. Use the least amount of glue possible in the mix as it will serve as a sealer, keeping any stain or finish from penetrating into the sawdust or surrounding wood.

Using either type of putty, allow the putty to mound slightly higher than the surface of the wood, as shrinkage will occur as the putty dries. When dry, simply sand the putty flush and apply your finish.

bottom in place and nail it up through the bottom. Next, slip the sub-top into place inside the case, under the top, and attach it to the top using screws. This sub-top builds up the front edge of the case to support the top moulding.

After a dry test fit, assemble the drawer dividers using glue and one or two strategically placed brads. Then

slide the drawer assembly into place in the case, using only glue.

While letting the case sit clamped-up for about an hour, mill the material for the top and bottom mouldings. Using the provided patterns on page 92, mark, then cut out the bracket feet patterns on the lower mouldings. The lower mouldings also have a decorative detail routed onto the top edge: Cut

Four ¼" dadoes are cut in each side to hold the drawer dividers. I like to use a trim router for this step, and also a template guide with a straight bit and piece of scrap wood as a straightedge.

I switched bits and routers, then cut a dado for the bottom in each side and a stopped rabbet on the back edge of each side to hold the ⅝" back boards in place.

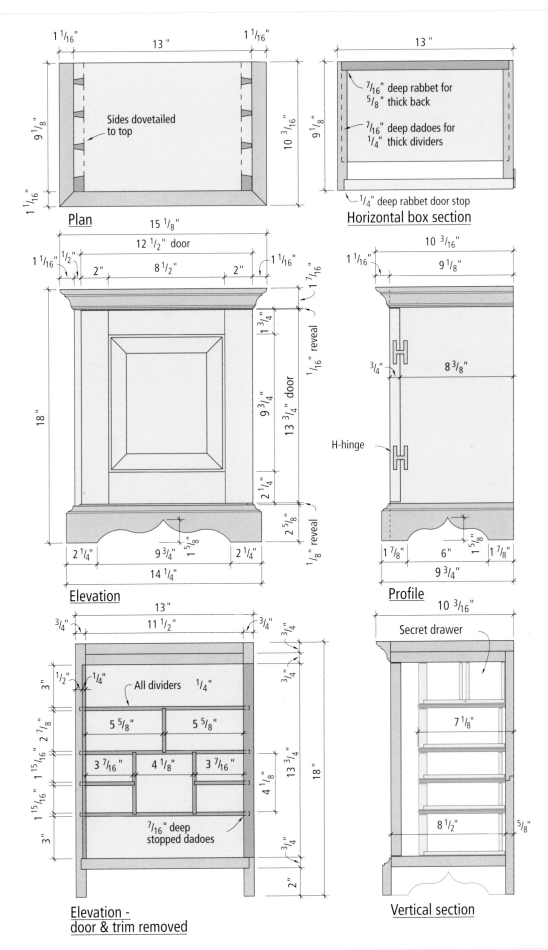

1 1/16"   13"   1 1/16"

9 1/8"

10 3/16"

1 1/16"

Sides dovetailed to top

Plan

13"

7/16" deep rabbet for 5/8" thick back

7/16" deep dadoes for 1/4" thick dividers

9 1/8"

1/4" deep rabbet door stop

Horizontal box section

15 1/8"

12 1/2" door

1 1/16" 1/2"   2"   8 1/2"   2"   1 1/16"

1 7/16"

1 3/4"

1/16" reveal

18"

9 3/4"

13 3/4" door

2 1/4"

2 5/8" reveal

1/8" reveal

2 1/4"   9 3/4"   1 5/8"   2 1/4"

14 1/4"

Elevation

10 3/16"

1 1/16"   9 1/8"

3/4"

8 3/8"

H-hinge

1 7/8"   6"   1 5/8"   1 7/8"

9 3/4"

Profile

13"

3/4"   11 1/2"   3/4"

3/4"

3/4"

3/4"

1/2"   1/4"

3"

All dividers   1/4"

2 7/8"

5 5/8"   5 5/8"

1 15/16"   1 15/16"

3 7/16"   4 1/8"   3 7/16"

13 3/4"

18"

4 1/8"

4 1/8"

1 15/16"

3"

7/16" deep stopped dadoes

3/4"

2"

Elevation - door & trim removed

10 3/16"

Secret drawer

7 1/8"

8 1/2"   5/8"

Vertical section

this next. The upper moulding uses a double-ogee design to form a miniature crown. See the diagrams to help match these patterns on your case. With the moulding shaped, miter the corners and attach them to the case using small brads. Nail directly through the moulding into the case. Cut the front mouldings to fit first, then work back from the corners to get the side mouldings the proper length. Set the brad nails below the wood surface, then use a matching putty to fill the holes.

The back for the case is made from two interlocking shiplapped poplar boards. The grain runs horizontally and the shiplapped joint is horizontal and falls somewhere near the center of the back. Cut the pieces and mill the rabbets to form the shiplapping, but leave the back loose until after finishing the piece. It's hard enough to finish the small drawer divider spaces.

The drawers use straightforward, traditional half-blind dovetails. Use poplar for all the parts except the fronts, which are walnut. See "Traditional Dovetailed Drawers" on page 92 for details.

The door is last. My fall-back door was a frame-and-panel design built

pennsylvania spice box **inches**

CASE

No.	Item	Dimensions T W L	Material	Comments
2	Sides	$3/4 \times 9^{1}/8 \times 18$	Walnut	
1	Bottom	$3/4 \times 8^{1}/2 \times 12^{1}/4$	Walnut	
1	Top	$3/4 \times 9^{1}/8 \times 13$	Walnut	
1	Sub-top	$3/4 \times 8^{1}/2 \times 11^{1}/2$	Walnut	
3	Horiz. dividers	$1/4 \times 6^{1}/2 \times 12^{3}/8$	Walnut	
2	Horiz. dividers	$1/4 \times 6^{1}/2 \times 4$	Walnut	
2	Vert. dividers	$1/4 \times 6^{1}/2 \times 4^{3}/8$	Walnut	
1	Vert. divider	$1/4 \times 6^{1}/2 \times 3^{1}/8$	Walnut	
1	Back	$5/8 \times 12^{3}/8 \times 17^{1}/4$	Poplar	Shiplapped
1	Top moulding	$1^{1}/16 \times 1^{7}/16 \times 44$	Walnut	
1	Bottom moulding	$5/8 \times 2^{5}/8 \times 36$	Walnut	

DRAWERS

No.	Item	Dimensions T W L	Material	Comments
1	Bottom front †	$5/8 \times 3 \times 11^{1}/2$	Walnut	
1	Center front †	$5/8 \times 4^{1}/8 \times 4^{1}/8$	Walnut	
4	Small fronts †	$5/8 \times 1^{15}/16 \times 3^{7}/16$	Walnut	
2	Split fronts †	$5/8 \times 2^{7}/8 \times 5^{5}/8$	Walnut	
1	Top front †	$5/8 \times 3 \times 11^{1}/2$	Walnut	
18	Sides	$1/4$" thick x (front width-$1/4$") wide x $5^{3}/4$"long		
9	Bottoms	$1/4$" thick x 6" wide x (length of front) long		
9	Backs	$1/4$" thick x (front width-$1/4$") wide x (length of front) long		

DOORS

No.	Item	Dimensions T W L	Material	Comments
1	Top rail	$3/4 \times 1^{3}/4 \times 11$	Walnut	$1^{1}/4$" TBE
1	Bottom rail	$3/4 \times 2^{1}/4 \times 11$	Walnut	$1^{1}/4$" TBE
2	Stiles	$3/4 \times 2 \times 13^{3}/4$	Walnut	
1	Panel	$5/8 \times 9^{1}/8 \times 10^{3}/8$	Walnut	$5/16$" TAS

TBE = Tenon on both ends; TAS = tenons all sides
*Door width nominal, trimmed to fit after assembly.
†Drawer front sizes fit openings exactly. Trim to fit once your case is assembled.

The door is fit into a recess on the right side. I made this recess by first running the side on edge over the table saw to define the top and bottom of the recess. Then I reset the saw, ran the blade height down below the surface of the table and slowly raised the blade into the piece while it was running. Push the piece through the saw to the end of the cut. The waste is connected by small pieces of wood and can be cut free simply with a handsaw.

pennsylvania spice box **millimeters**

CASE

No.	Item	Dimensions T W L	Material	Comments
2	Sides	19 x 232 x 457	Walnut	
1	Bottom	19 x 216 x 311	Walnut	
1	Top	19 x 232 x 330	Walnut	
1	Sub-top	19 x 216 x 292	Walnut	
3	Horiz. dividers	6 x 165 x 315	Walnut	
2	Horiz. dividers	6 x 65 x 102	Walnut	
2	Vert. dividers	6 x 165 x 112	Walnut	
1	Vert. divider	6 x 165 x 79	Walnut	
1	Back	16 x 315 x 438	Poplar	Shiplapped
1	Top moulding	27 x 36 x 1118	Walnut	
1	Bottom moulding	16 x 67 x 914	Walnut	

DRAWERS

No.	Item	Dimensions T W L	Material	Comments
1	Bottom front †	16 x 76 x 292	Walnut	
1	Center front †	16 x 105 x 105	Walnut	
4	Small fronts †	16 x 49 x 87	Walnut	
2	Split fronts †	16 x 73 x 143	Walnut	
1	Top front †	16 x 76 x 292	Walnut	
18	Sides	6mm thick x (front width-6mm) wide x 146mm long		
9	Bottoms	6mm thick x 152mm wide x (length of front) long		
9	Backs	6mm thick x (front width-6mm) wide x (length of front) long		

DOORS

No.	Item	Dimensions T W L	Material	Comments
1	Top rail	19 x 45 x 279	Walnut	32mm TBE
1	Bottom rail	19 x 57 x 279	Walnut	32mm TBE
2	Stiles	19 x 51 x 349	Walnut	
1	Panel	16 x 232 x 264	Walnut	8mm TAS

TBE = Tenon on both ends; TAS = tenons all sides
*Door width nominal, trimmed to fit after assembly.
† Drawer front sizes fit openings exactly. Trim to fit once your case is assembled.

with haunched mortise-and-tenon joinery. While I don't want to set you up for failure, I'd definitely make sure I had enough walnut for the frame and panel door in case things don't work out as planned.

To make the door, cut your rails, stiles and panel to rough size. Select stock for the panel with some nice figure to make the door really special. Start by running a $^3/_{16}$" beading profile on the inside front edge of each piece. The inside edge of the bead should roll into the panel once it's in place. Next cut a $^1/_4$"-wide × $^3/_8$"-deep groove down the center of the inside edge of each door stile and rail. Then make a $^1/_4$" × 1" mortise, $1^1/_4$" deep at the top and bottom of each stile, $^1/_4$" in from each end. The $^1/_4$" width should center on the previously made groove, and the depth of the mortise should include the depth of the groove itself.

Next, set up your table saw to make the $^1/_4$"-thick × $1^1/_4$"-long tenons on both ends of the door rails. The tenon is again centered on the piece. Now miter the beaded profile. Tip your table saw's blade to 45°, and with the rail resting on the inside edge, use your miter gauge to notch the inside corners, $1^1/_4$"

With the case dovetails cut and the bottom bracket for the feet cut out, you're ready to assemble. The dovetails are simple, and the cleverness of the design shows as you're able to nail the bottom in place in the rabbets, through the access made by cutting out the feet brackets.

TRADITIONAL DOVETAILED DRAWERS

Not only is the construction of the drawers traditional, the secret hiding spaces are as well. The spices kept in these boxes were already considered valuable, but the original builders wanted to make it possible to store even more valuable items undetected. Behind both second-tier drawers are secret drawers. It's a nice touch, but it's your choice whether to add them or not. The sizes given in the Materials List are for full-depth drawers in those spaces. You can change the dimensions as you like to add your own secrets.

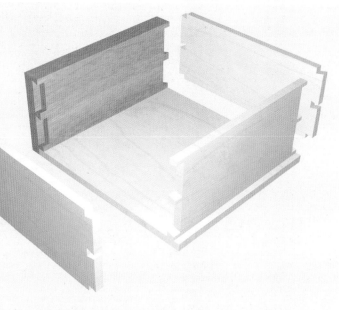

Half-blind dovetails mate the fronts and sides, and through-dovetails mate the backs and sides of the drawers. The bottoms are simply tacked on to the sides and back using brads. This method of attaching the bottoms will prove sufficient to carry the amount of weight in these small drawers.

Each drawer uses three dovetail pins per joint, and all that I made were hand cut. Start by cutting the drawer fronts to fit in each of the spaces with about $\frac{1}{16}$" clearance on all sides. With all the fronts cut, set up a router to cut a $\frac{1}{4}$"-high × $\frac{3}{8}$" rabbet on the inside bottom edge of each front. The sides should align with the top of the rabbet, so go ahead and lay out your dovetails on the fronts, sides and backs.

With all the dovetails cut and fit, cut the bottoms for each drawer to width, but leave them a little long. The length of the drawer bottom will serve as a stop against the case back to keep the drawer fronts aligned properly. The exception to this applies

when making any secret drawers. Leave a longer bottom on the secret drawer, but make the front drawer bottom flush to the back. Assemble the drawers with glue, then tack the bottoms in place using a few small brads.

Trim the drawer bottoms so everything aligns in front nicely, then add the simple screw-on knobs to the drawers. Follow the same finishing technique that was used for the main case and you're ready to start filling up your spice box.

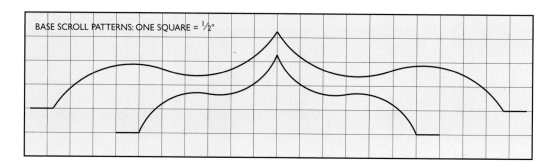

BASE SCROLL PATTERNS: ONE SQUARE = $\frac{1}{2}$"

With the drawer dividers assembled and installed, it's ready for the moulding. The top moulding was made using a Roman ogee bit in two steps, then nailed in place. The lower moulding is cut to provide the bracket base design using the scaled patterns provided on page 92, then an attractive profile is run on the top edge. The rest is simply mitering and nailing in place.

in from each end and at a height of $^3/_{16}$". While the blade is set to 45°, make a similar cut on the two stiles, set at $^3/_{16}$" high and starting $1^3/_4$" in from the top end of each stile, and $2^1/_4$" in from the bottom end.

Reset the blade to 90°, and by running each stile on end with the outside edge against the rip fence, trim $^3/_{16}$" from the inside edge of each stile, up to the height of the previously cut 45° miter.

With the tenon formed, it's time to make it a haunched tenon. Using your miter gauge, notch the outside edge of each door rail tenon 1" in (including the blade thickness) and $^1/_4$" high. Then use your rip fence to cut away the tenon waste on either side of the rail tenons, leaving the appropriate width tenon to fit in the mortises in the stiles. You should be able to dry fit the door together now to check your joints.

I used a panel-raising bit in my router table to shape the door panel. Allow the appropriate thickness at the edge of the panel for it to fit into the grooves in the stiles and rails. The flat of the panel will extend $^1/_8$" beyond the front surface of the door, while the back surface of the panel will fit exact-

The drawers are built to match the traditional style of the original piece, with the backs attached in through-dovetails to the sides, and the fronts attached to the sides with half-blind dovetails. The bottoms are simply nailed onto the sides, which would be a poor idea for anything larger than these drawers. Though the Materials List doesn't call out the pieces for it, I added a very typical secret drawer behind one of the drawers. Read "Traditional Dovetailed Drawers" on page 92 for more information on the secret drawers.

Detail of Door Construction

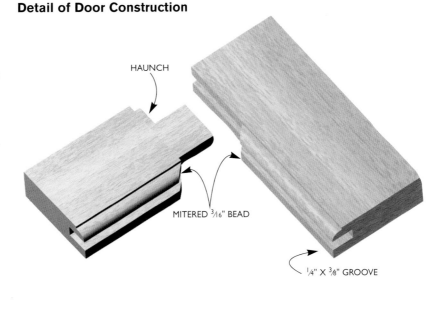

HAUNCH

MITERED $^3/_{16}$" BEAD

$^1/_4$" X $^3/_8$" GROOVE

Take your time fitting and attaching the door to the case. Because it's inset on three sides, and traditional hinges don't allow for much slop, you need to get it right the first time.

ly into the groove and form a ¼" recess. Assemble the door using glue in the mortise-and-tenon joints, but allow the panel to float loose in the grooves. I added squared pegs to the joints, drilling all the way through the door at the center of each tenon and sanding the pegs flush to the surface of the door.

The door is hung on the case using an H-shaped hinge that's screwed into the right-hand edge of the door and the right side of the case. The lock set requires a recess routed into the back of the door. Since each of the locks are fairly individual, use the actual lock to determine the appropriate size for the recess. The same goes for the recess required in the left-side piece to accept the bolt from the lock.

To finish the piece I filled the grain with a paste filler then applied a couple of coats of blond shellac to bring out the beauty of the walnut. Though there are lots of little pieces, this is a very pleasing box when finished. All the basics of a larger piece, but it fits on your table. See page 95 for the fancy door.

Supplies

Horton Brasses Inc. 800-754-9127 or
www.horton-brasses.com
1 - Lock - #LK-11
1 - Escutcheon - #H-121
11 - Knobs - #H-42
2 - Hinges - #HH2, the 2¼" versions

inlay door
with a router

How to make an amazing inlay door
for the Pennsylvania Spice Box using
your router and band saw.

I'd never tried anything like inlay when I came across the image of a great-looking 18th century spice box. The image struck me and I stopped to consider the skill required to make the piece. When I started thinking harder I realized that the inlay was almost entirely designed with geometric shapes. While I'm no artist, I can handle math and geometry. The more I thought about it, the more I realized it was within my grasp.

The previous project shows how to build the basic cabinet and a frame-and-panel door for the piece. This time I'm going to show you how to tackle inlay with some jigs, some patience and tools you likely already have in your shop.

Which Comes First: The Inlay or the Recesses?
I debated whether it made more sense to cut the ⅛"-deep recesses in the door first and then fit the inlay in

place, or to start by making the inlay. In practicing on a piece of inlay I realized that even though I was working toward achieving a specific width, it wasn't easy to end up at the size I'd planned. So I decided to make all the inlay parts first, then cut the recesses to match.

The pictures on this and the following pages provide most of the instruction for this project, but there are some additional general observations that will prove useful. One of the steps toward a good-looking piece of inlay is to have the different wood types butt against each other with a nearly invisible gap. Because of this, fitting individual pieces by careful hand sanding is critical. That's where the patience comes in.

A light touch proves beneficial when gluing the banding together. If too

much glue is applied and left in place, your inlay will show glue lines when finished. Take it easy with the glue. It's only holding an $\frac{1}{8}$" piece of wood in place, and it doesn't take much.

The inlay pieces are made using cherry, tiger maple and walnut. Straight-grain pieces are easier to work with, especially with the vining patterns, but the tiger maple pattern can also be very attractive in some areas. And in the chevron pattern I used quarter-sawn grain — or side grain on a flat sawn board — to make the inlay more dramatic. Choose your wood carefully, and make a few extra pieces, just in case.

The door itself is a $\frac{3}{4}$" × $12\frac{1}{2}$" × $13\frac{3}{4}$" walnut panel. Start with an over-

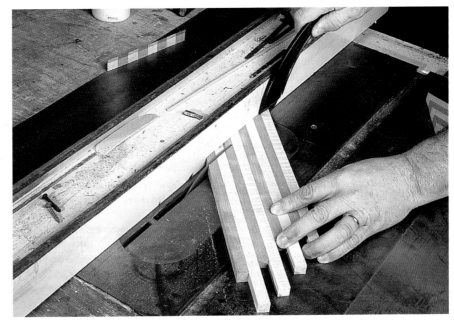

The first inlay to make is the outer frame. Start by gluing up eight $\frac{35}{64}$"-wide × $\frac{3}{4}$"-thick strips, angling the glue-up to anticipate the 45° cuts that will follow. When the glue dries, cut a 45° miter on one end, then set your table saw to cut $\frac{5}{16}$"-wide strips. Be careful, and use a push stick.

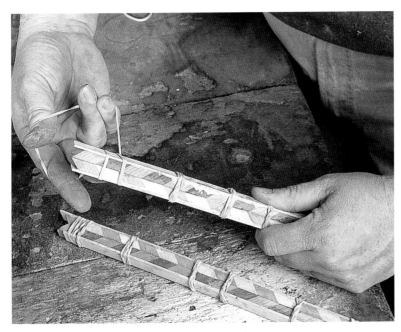

To form the chevron banding, glue the previously cut strips together, alternating the color pattern. At the same time, glue the $\frac{1}{16}$" outer striping in place to the outer edges. This will bring the finished pattern to the final $\frac{3}{4}$" width. I ripped the striping off a $\frac{3}{4}$"-thick, 4"-wide block on the table saw, allowing the $\frac{1}{16}$" piece to be the fall-off of the cut for safety. Some sanding on the mating faces — and using only the amount of glue necessary — will keep the glue line as small as possible.

After the glue-up is dry, set up a fence on the band saw to make a resaw cut, slightly thicker than $\frac{1}{8}$". I started with both outside faces of the inlay sanded flat and cut the two outside surfaces from the block. I resanded the faces of the piece that was left, and made two more cuts. Each piece should yield four lengths of banding. The smooth face on each length is the side that I glued down to the panel.

routers. I do recommend that you take a few minutes to tune up your band saw before the project. You'll be resawing small, $\frac{1}{8}$"-thick pieces on that machine and you want it to cut straight, square and smooth.

I didn't take any pictures of the final sanding process. Once you get all the inlay pieces in place in the door it looks like a little topographical map with bumps and ridges all over the place. When you get ready to sand, take it easy. If you start in with too aggressive a grit you will leave sanding marks in some of the delicate, cross-grain inlay pieces and you could pull something loose. Start with a fine grit sandpaper. I used a random-orbit sander to level the door, but if you do the same, be patient.

With the inlays made, lay out the pattern on the door front. The first step is to cut the circle pattern. I used a shop-made circle-cutting jig (show on page 101 — though you can also purchase one), making the 1"-wide recess $\frac{1}{8}$" deep in two overlapping passes using a $\frac{3}{4}$" straight bit. Start with the outside dimension, then adjust the jig inward to the inner diameter.

For the next step I chose to make a simple 2×4 frame and used a bit with a top-mounted bearing to create the outer border recess. This ensures that the corners will meet accurately. I used a $\frac{3}{4}$"-wide straight bit to make the cut with a single pass. After the cut, use a chisel to square out the corners.

To make the mating arc inlays in the corners I used a template guide and trim router with a $\frac{1}{16}$"-wide bit. I made the template from a $\frac{1}{2}$" piece of scrap plywood. The inlay runs out from the outer banding. Use the diagram on page 99 to make your own template so your cut starts right at the corner. The notches at the ends of the arc will help you start and stop your cuts.

The center mating arcs are made using the same bit and template guide, but a new plywood jig. Note that I used center lines struck on the door front to orient my template jig.

With all the recesses cut, it's time to put the inlay in place. I started with the outer chevron banding. Above, I'm marking the center of each run to reverse the direction of the chevrons. This actually makes it easier to glue in the pattern.

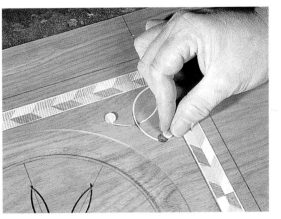

Finally, glue the center ring inlay in place. The trick here is getting the four quarters of the circle to the correct lengths so they mate exactly, with almost no visible joint.

To make the banding for the corner arcs, set your table saw to once again slice $^1/_{16}$" strips from a larger piece. Then carefully slice the strip to a little over $^1/_8$" thick. A straightedge and utility knife will serve well here. Then add a little glue and press them into the recess. Make some extra strips in case some snap. I used tiger maple, which is pretty brittle. Holly would have been easier to work with.

For the "berry" designs I used a $^3/_8$" plug cutter to make several $^1/_8$"-thick dots. Carefully glue these in place. The berries in the center of the pattern are created the same way.

Circle-Cutting Jig

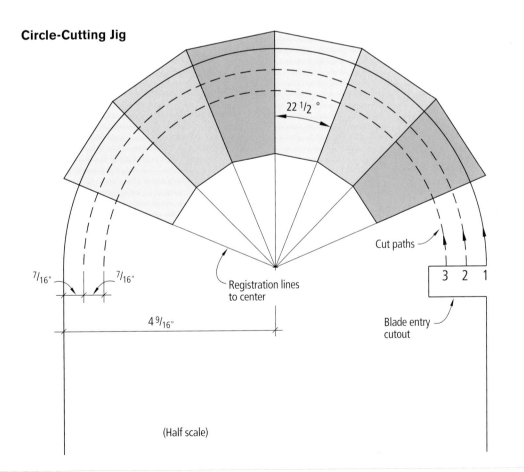

22 $^1/_2$ °

Cut paths

3 2 1

$^7/_{16}$" $^7/_{16}$"

Registration lines to center

Blade entry cutout

4 $^9/_{16}$"

(Half scale)

craftsman **wall shelf**

Learn to make through-mortises using a template and a router as you construct this simple and sturdy shelf.

L ike most woodworkers, I try not to reinvent the wheel every time I build a project. Instead, I search through my library and back issues of woodworking magazines to see if I can find what I'm looking for. I usually don't find exactly what I want, but if it's close, it's easy to modify a dimension or decorative feature. So I was quite surprised when I started looking around for a Craftsman-style wall shelf and came up empty. Further digging revealed that the Craftsman folks of yesteryear didn't use them. Not because they didn't have knick-knacks, but because they relied on built-in shelving units and large side-boards or buffets to store and display their cherished collectibles.

Undaunted, I dusted off my drafting table and put pencil to paper. Designing a wall shelf like this was fairly straightforward, as I had a rough idea of the dimensions I needed and knew I

wanted three shelves approximately 30" long. As I worked, I incorporated three classic Craftsman-style details into the wall shelf: shallow, graceful curves; the corbel (the distinctive curved shape at the bottom of the sides); and the honesty of through-mortise-and-tenon joints. Although quartersawn oak is a trademark of Craftsman-style furniture, I chose cherry instead for two reasons. First, quartersawn oak is highly figured and I wanted the items displayed to catch the eye rather than the shelf itself. Second, I was looking for a formal, dignified look. I've always felt that cherry adds a touch of elegance to any piece.

Once I was comfortable with the design and had worked out the majority of the details, I made a quick mock-up to get a better feel of how the curves would work together and to better visualize the finished piece. For more details, see "Crude but Effective Mock-up" on page 106.

Construction

To build the Craftsman-style wall shelf, start by cutting the parts to size according to the Materials List. There are only seven parts to the shelf: two identical sides, three identical shelves and a top and bottom bracket. The sides and shelves are ⁷⁄₈" thick and the brackets are ¾". As you cut the parts to size, set some of the thicknessed scraps aside for test cuts later.

Mortises

The biggest challenge to building the wall shelf is cutting the mortises for the shelf tenons. Because these are through-tenons and will be highly visible, I decided it would be best to build a simple router jig for added accuracy (see the drawing on page 107). The jig is just a piece of ¼"-thick hardboard with cleats screwed around the edges

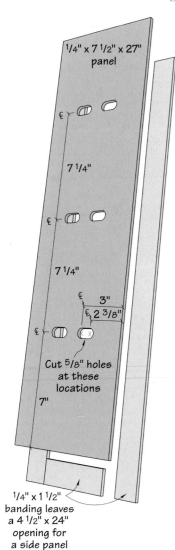

1/4" x 7 1/2" x 27"
panel

7 1/4"

7 1/4"

3"
2 3/8"

Cut ⁵⁄₈" holes
at these
locations

7"

1/4" x 1 1/2"
banding leaves
a 4 1/2" x 24"
opening for
a side panel

Cleats screwed around the perimeter of the mortising jig capture a side piece for routing the mortises.

A plunge router plus a mortising jig equals precision mortises — something that's paramount when the mortises are through and the tenons are exposed.

To guarantee the mortise corners end up perfectly vertical, clamp a scrap of wood flush with the edge of the mortise to guide the chisel.

No.	Ltr.	Item	Dimensions T W L	Material
2	A	Sides	$7/8 \times 4^1/2 \times 24$	Cherry
3	B	Shelves	$7/8 \times 4^1/2 \times 30^*$	Cherry
1	C	Top bracket	$3/4 \times 3^1/2 \times 28^3/4^*$	Cherry
1	D	Bottom bracket	$3/4 \times 3^1/2 \times 28^3/4^*$	Cherry

* measurement includes tenon length on both ends

craftsman wall shelf **millimeters**

No.	Ltr.	Item	Dimensions T W L	Material
2	A	Sides	$22 \times 115 \times 610$	Cherry
3	B	Shelves	$22 \times 115 \times 762^*$	Cherry
1	C	Top bracket	$19 \times 89 \times 730^*$	Cherry
1	D	Bottom bracket	$19 \times 89 \times 730^*$	Cherry

* measurement includes tenon length on both ends

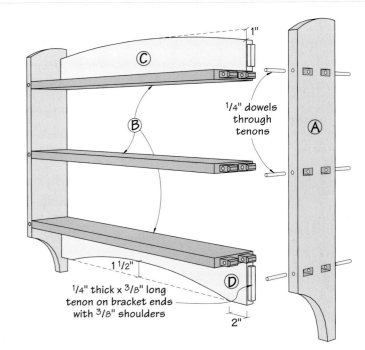

1"

¼" dowels through tenons

¼" thick x ³/8" long tenon on bracket ends with ³/8" shoulders

1 1/2"

2"

to hold a side piece in perfect position. Pairs of slots for the mortises in the hardboard are sized to accept a $5/8$" OD, $17/32$" ID template guide bushing for the router. This bushing can be used with a $1/2$"-diameter straight bit or spiral-end mill bit. I drilled the holes in the hardboard with a $5/8$" brad-point bit and removed the waste between the holes with a sharp chisel.

To use the router jig, fit it over a side and slide a scrap of plywood underneath because you'll be routing all the way through the side. Using a plunge router, take a series of light cuts, blowing out the chips from the mortise after every pass. Continue until you've cut all the way through. Then move on to the next mortise.

All that's left is to square up the round corners of each through-mortise with a chisel. Although you can do this with a conventional beveled-edge chisel, a corner chisel will make quick work of the job. Since I lean heavily towards the Craftsman style, it was easy to justify the modest cost of this fine tool. To ensure the corner cuts are perfectly vertical, clamp a guide block flush with the edge of the mortise and press the corner chisel firmly against it as you strike the chisel with a hammer.

There are a couple more mortises to cut on each side piece — these accept the tenons on the ends of the top and

A drum sander fitted in the drill press makes quick work of smoothing the corbel on the bottom, and the gentle curve on top of each side piece.

bottom brackets. Since these aren't through-mortises, you needn't use a jig. Instead, lay them out directly on the sides making sure to bookmatch them as shown. To cut these mortises, I used a $1/4$" mortising bit in the drill press and clamped a fence on the back edge for accuracy.

Side Shapes

With the mortises complete, use the drawing on page 107 to make a pattern for the sides out of $1/4$" hardboard. Carefully cut this out with a jigsaw or band saw and sand the edges smooth. Then place the pattern on each side piece and trace around it with a pencil. Now you can cut the sides to shape and sand the edges smooth.

5/8" 1 1/8"

3/16"

1"

1 1/8"

5/8"

1/2"

3/16"

1/8"

1"

Chamfers

CRUDE BUT EFFECTIVE MOCK-UP

If you've ever built a project that you designed only to be disappointed with the final proportions or the decorative details, consider making a crude but effective mock-up before cutting into your precious stack of hardwood. I unintentionally started using foam board years ago when I was rummaging around the shop one day looking for inexpensive scrap to mock up a project. I stumbled across a battered piece of $\frac{3}{4}$"-thick foam insulation board and thought, "Why not?" It cuts easily by hand or with power tools, you can screw it together temporarily with drywall screws and it's really cheap. The only problem working with it is getting past the color — the rather hideous pink shown here or the other common color, pale blue. On the mock-up I built for the wall shelf, I was playing around with the back curves on the top piece trying to figure out what looked best. I cut a couple of different foam pieces and tried each in turn. It only took a few minutes, and it's a great way to lock in a troublesome detail. Ever since that first foam board mock-up, I try to keep at least one sheet of $\frac{1}{2}$" and one sheet of $\frac{3}{4}$" foam board stocked in my shop.

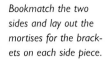

Bookmatch the two sides and lay out the mortises for the brackets on each side piece.

The shoulders for tenons on the shelves are easily cut on a table saw that's fitted with a dado blade.

Clamping a tall support fence to your miter gauge will make cutting the twin tenons a safe and easy operation.

Foam insulation board is an inexpensive mock-up material that allows you to quickly visualize what a project will look like before cutting any wood.

Shelf Tenons

When the sides are complete, turn your attention to the shelves. Basically all there is to do here is to cut the tenons on the ends to fit the mortises in the sides. Since the sides are $\frac{7}{8}$" thick, I made the tenons 1" long so they'd protrude through the $\frac{7}{8}$"-thick sides by $\frac{1}{8}$". I cut the twin tenons in two steps. First, with a dado blade in the table saw set for a shallow cut, cut an equal amount off each face to create the shoulders, leaving a $\frac{1}{2}$"-thick tenon — this is where those scrap pieces come in handy. Then, with each shelf on end and a tall support piece attached to the miter gauge, make the end and middle shoulder cuts to form the twin tenons.

Here again, use the scrap pieces and sneak up on the perfect fit. Take your time and test the fit often — what you're looking for is a friction fit — if you even think about reaching for a hammer to persuade the joint to go together, it's too tight. Stop and take a little more off, a finely tuned shoulder plane is excellent for this. Finally, to soften the ends of the tenons and help them slide more easily into the mortises, I chamfered the ends with a block plane.

Brackets

The last two pieces of the wall shelf are the top and bottom brackets. Each has a graceful curve and tenons cut on the ends to fit into the matching mortises

A friction fit of the tenons in the mortises is what you're looking for. You should feel just a slight resistance as you slide the pieces together.

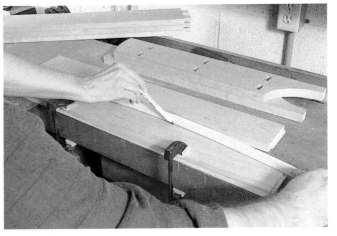

The graceful curves on the top and bottom brackets can be laid out with the aid of a helper by tracing along a bent strip of thin wood.

A keyhole bit fitted in a handheld router and run along a guide block is an easy way to attach the shelf to a wall.

that were cut into the sides. Once you've cut the tenons, lay out the curves by bending a thin strip of wood into a graceful curve and have a helper trace the outline on each bracket. The old boat maker's adage "If it looks fair, it is fair," certainly applies here. After you've laid out the curves, cut out the shapes and sand the edges smooth.

Assembly

Before assembling the Craftsman-style wall shelf, there are a couple things to do. First soften the edges by routing or planing an ⅛" chamfer on all edges except for the top edges of the bottom bracket, the bottom edges of the top bracket and the back edges of the shelves. Next sand all the pieces. This is a habit that's worth developing — you'll save yourself a lot of frustration in the long run trying to sand inaccessible spots.

To assemble the wall shelf, first make a dry run. Assemble all the pieces and clamp the shelf together without glue to make sure there won't be any surprises. Then carefully disassemble the shelf and apply a small amount of white glue — don't use yellow glue here, it sets up too quickly — to the tenons on the shelves and the tenons on the top and bottom bracket. Also, apply a thin bead of glue to the bottom edge of the top bracket and the top edge of the bottom bracket. Working

quickly, slide the shelves and top and bottom brackets into one side piece. Then position the remaining side piece and apply clamps from side to side. You'll also want to clamp the top and bottom brackets along their lengths to their respective shelves.

After the glue dries remove the clamps, and pin the shelves to the sides with short lengths of dowel for added strength. I drilled 2"-deep holes from both the front and back of each side piece to allow the dowel to pass completely through each tenon to lock it securely in place. A dollop of glue on each end and a few raps of a hammer is all it takes. You can pare off any protruding dowel with a sharp chisel. Finally, I routed a pair of keyhole slots in the back to hang the shelf and applied two coats of satin polyurethane. Mounted on the wall, this Craftsman-style shelf graces any home and proudly displays your favorite collection of pottery, knickknacks — even antique tools.

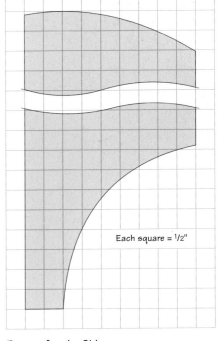

Each square = ½"

Pattern for the Sides

modern
occasional table

A good project for an aspiring beginner, this table squeezes a bit of storage from a place that is usually wasted.

There is space and need in almost everyone's home for an occasional table. But to sweeten the concept, we've come up with a dual purpose for this design. Every family room has those certain items you need only occasionally (is that where the name came from?), but there's never a good place to keep them. You know, the remote control you rarely use, the pocket dictionary, or the coasters for when company's around. Well, lift the top off this table and you've uncovered a storage space for those occasionally needed items.

Getting Started on the Legs

Construction begins by cutting out the parts according to the Materials List. Start with the tapered legs. There are many methods for doing this, but the simplest is just laying out the taper on each leg, cutting it out with a band saw and planing the taper with a bench plane.

First determine which sides of the legs will face out, choosing the best figure for those faces. The tapers are only on the two inside faces of each leg. To keep the legs correctly oriented, place the legs as they will be on the finished table, then hold them together and mark a diamond across the intersection

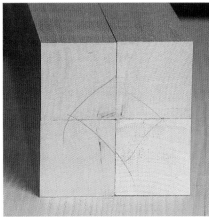

The diamond marked on the tops of the four legs will always allow you to recognize the inside and outside faces of the legs.

To mark the foot of each leg, a combination square is used to locate the 1" mark. I use a pen when laying out these measurements so they won't fade or be easily obscured during the clean-up process on the tapers.

of all four legs at the top.

Next, mark each leg on the inside face (where the aprons will butt against) at $4^5/_{16}$" and $4^{13}/_{16}$" down from the top. The $4^5/_{16}$" measurement is the location of the bottom edge of the apron, which leaves $^1/_{16}$" of the leg protruding above the top, adding a nice detail. The $4^{13}/_{16}$" measurement is the starting location of the leg taper.

Now move to the bottoms of the legs and using a combination square, mark a 1" square on each leg, measuring from the outside corner. This indicates where the inside tapers will end on each leg. Connect the marks from the top to the bottom of the legs, then cut the tapers on a band saw, cutting as close to the line as you can. To smooth out the band saw cut, use a bench plane and a bit of muscle to remove the rough-sawn edge.

The term "occasional table" implies that this table won't be expected to carry a lot of weight. In that spirit, the joinery doesn't have to be extraordinarily strong. Two #20 biscuits in each joint provide plenty of strength for the base. The $^1/_4$" plywood bottom screwed in place will add to the base's strength.

Set up the joinery by marking each leg $2^9/_{16}$" from the top (the center point for the aprons). Adjust the biscuit joiner to space two biscuits evenly in the thickness of each apron and to position the aprons flush to the legs.

After cutting the biscuit joints, set up a router to run a $^1/_4$" × $^5/_8$"-wide rab-

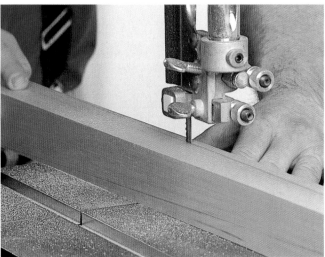

The simplest way to cut the tapers is on a band saw. Cut as close to the line as you can, leaving a little extra to the outside of the line. A bench plane does a nice job of cleaning up the tapers after being band sawn, but there's no sense in leaving too much work.

bet in the bottom edge of the aprons for the bottom. With the rabbets cut, start assembling the base by gluing the short aprons between the legs. Dealing with fewer clamps on any procedure makes the glue-up easier.

Check for square on each glued-up end by measuring from the top corner of one leg to the bottom corner of the other, making sure the measurements are equal. After about an hour, glue up the rest of the base, again checking the

base for square on the sides and across the width and length of the apron. For the loose top to fit accurately, you have to be on the money.

Take the time to wipe off any glue that you see before it dries. The inside of the table gets finished, so you have to keep squeeze-out to a minimum.

Cut out a $^1/_4$" bottom to fit the dimensions between the rabbets in the aprons. To let the bottom fit in place correctly, notch the corners around the

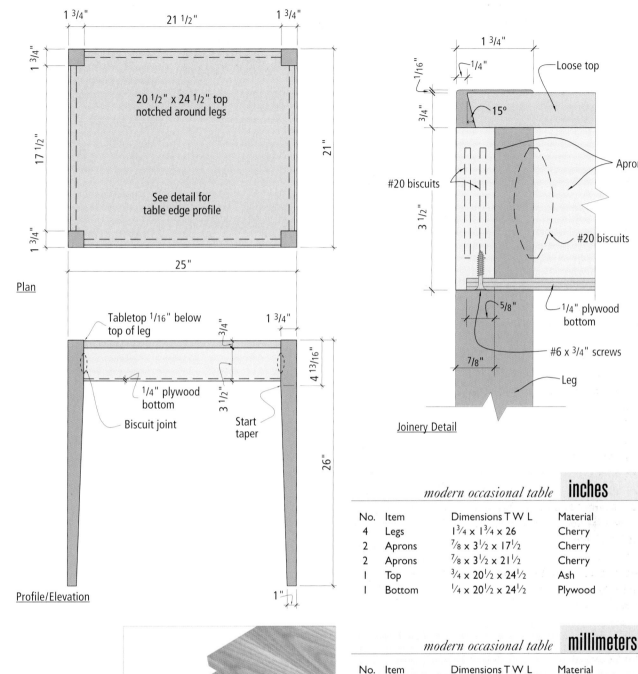

1 3/4"

21 1/2"

1 3/4"

1 3/4"

17 1/2"

21"

1 3/4"

20 1/2" x 24 1/2" top
notched around legs

See detail for
table edge profile

25"

Plan

Tabletop 1/16" below
top of leg

3/4"

1 3/4"

1/4" plywood
bottom

Biscuit joint

3 1/2"

Start
taper

4 13/16"

26"

Profile/Elevation

1"

1 3/4"

1/16"

1/4"

Loose top

3/4"

15°

Apron

#20 biscuits

3 1/2"

#20 biscuits

1/4" plywood
bottom

5/8"

#6 x 3/4" screws

7/8"

Leg

Joinery Detail

modern occasional table	**inches**		
No.	Item	Dimensions T W L	Material
4	Legs	1³/₄ x 1³/₄ x 26	Cherry
2	Aprons	⁷/₈ x 3¹/₂ x 17¹/₂	Cherry
2	Aprons	⁷/₈ x 3¹/₂ x 21¹/₂	Cherry
I	Top	³/₄ x 20¹/₂ x 24¹/₂	Ash
I	Bottom	¹/₄ x 20¹/₂ x 24¹/₂	Plywood

modern occasional table	**millimeters**		
No.	Item	Dimensions T W L	Material
4	Legs	45 x 45 x 660	Cherry
2	Aprons	22 x 89 x 445	Cherry
2	Aprons	22 x 89 x 546	Cherry
I	Top	19 x 521 x 623	Ash
I	Bottom	6 x 521 x 623	Plywood

legs using the band saw. Don't install the bottom until after finishing.

The last construction step is the top. I made mine from quartersawn ash to create an interesting contrast to the cherry base. The top's width was achieved by gluing up four thinner boards. The grain on quartersawn ash is so straight that it's hard to find the glue joints. After the top is glued up and dry, cut it to the same size as the outside dimensions of the table base, which is a bit bigger than the finished size of the top.

Referencing off the table base helps you cut accurate notches in the top. Mark the notch locations by laying the top upside down on a clean surface, then turn the base upside down and lay it on the top, flushing the corners. Mark the leg locations for the notches.

To notch the top using a table saw, clamp a $^3/_4$" spacer board to the rip fence about 3" back from the leading edge of the blade. Set the blade's height and the distance from the fence (including the blade) to the size of your notch and add $^1/_{16}$" to the cut to allow room for wood movement.

The top is run on edge against the saw's miter gauge. It's a good idea to add a sacrificial board to the miter gauge as well to add some extra height for support, and to back the top behind the notch to reduce tear-out. The top is pushed up to the spacer block on the fence, then pushed past the blade, holding the top tightly against the miter gauge. The spacer block allows you to properly align the piece for the cut, cut, but keeps the notch (once cut free) from binding between the blade and fence, causing a dangerous kickback. Check the fit of your top. To allow you to lift the top, it needs to be a little loose. Next, cut the bevels on the top's edges by setting your table saw's blade to 15°. Set the rip fence so the cut is almost flush to the top edge of the top, leaving about a $^1/_{32}$" flat on the edge. This cut will remove about $^1/_4$" off the underside of the edge. Re-

The double biscuits in the apron/leg joint will provide adequate strength for an occasional table. The biscuits are carefully located to keep the apron flush to the leg, while still providing even strength across the joint.

Notching the top on the table saw can be an easy process. Notice the gap between the top and the saw's rip fence. This is the space left when the top is pushed beyond the spacer block attached to the fence. The gap will keep the notched piece from binding. Also notice that the top is clamped to the miter gauge. This is a good idea to hold everything in place.

peat this cut on the other edges, then finish sand the top.

After sanding the base, apply a mix of boiled linseed oil and stain. The recipe is as follows: Mix $^1/_2$ teaspoon of Pratt and Lambert Tonetic Cherry Bark stain (S7441) and $^1/_2$ teaspoon of Minwax (#223) Colonial Maple stain with 4 ounces of boiled linseed oil. This gives the impression that the cherry's color is already darkened. The top gets no stain. Apply three coats of clear finish to the base, top and bottom. When the final coat is dry, screw in the bottom with some #6 × $^3/_4$" flathead screws.

european
telephone console

Keep your phone, phone books, keys and small umbrellas in order – all without taking up a single square inch of floor space in your front hall.

Being worldly woodworkers, the *Popular Woodworking* staff spends time checking out woodworking ideas from Britain, Australia and even Germany. It was in a German woodworking magazine called Selbst that we saw a similar entry hall stand. Its clean lines and utilitarian efficiency caught our eye, so we decided to give it a little American schooling and share it with our readers.

Two Triangles

I was able to get all the necessary parts (except the back) out of a 4' × 4' piece of cherry plywood. Start construction by ripping two 12½"-wide pieces from the sheet of plywood, then crosscut the pieces to 38" long. Next, strike a pencil line from one corner, 12" from what will be the back edge, and connect it to a point on the opposite corner, 1½" from the same back edge. Mark both pieces, making sure you have left- and right-facing pieces.

Head to the band saw with the two pieces and cut along the pencil line, leaving about an ⅛" wide of the line. Then take the two pieces to the jointer and trim the angled edge straight and fairly close (¹⁄₁₆") to the line. To make the two pieces identical, clamp them together, flushing up the back and top edges. Using a sharp bench plane, I made a few passes on the angled edge to even up the pieces.

Parts for the Middle

Grab what's left of your plywood sheet and rip an 11"-wide strip from it. From this 11" × 48"-long piece you'll be able to get the door, the kick, the two cleats and the shelf. Crosscut all the pieces except the shelf to size. The piece that is left is enough to make the shelf, but I turned the shelf so the grain would run longways to better match the veneer tape. Go ahead and cut the shelf to size now.

It's time to disguise the plywood as solid wood. The front and top edges of

IRON-ON WOOD

There are lots of reasons to use plywood in a project: cost, weight and even environmental considerations. But just because you aren't using solid wood you don't need to give up the look of solid wood. Iron-on veneer tape has been around for a long while, but it has sort of a "cheap" reputation. I'm here to tell you it's worth a look.

Available in a wide variety of wood species, veneer tape is actual wood veneer with a heat-sensitive adhesive applied to the back. With the heat of a household iron and a few simple tools you can turn a piece of plywood into a finished and attractive piece of wood.

Follow these steps for some tips to getting the best results from veneer tape.

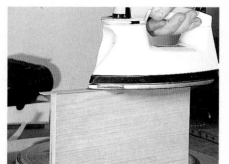

Since trying to use the iron to hold the tape in place as the glue dries just reheats the glue, switch to a simple block of wood. The chunk of poplar shown here works great. The bottom surface is sanded smooth and the edges are broken to avoid snagging or scratching. Simply apply pressure and make long passes over the edge for about 30 seconds. If you have a few pieces to veneer, set the first piece aside to let the glue cool.

Start with a piece of tape that's about 2" longer than the edge you are covering. Your iron should be on a cotton setting, with the steam turned off. Make sure the tape overhangs the edge evenly, then start ironing. Make long passes over the edge, not stopping in one place for any length of time, applying heat evenly. The tape will start to curl up a little as the glue melts.

To trim the edge, start by carefully bending over the ends until the veneer breaks. Make sure you apply pressure to the end of the attached veneer so it doesn't splinter back onto the visible edge. Then pull the "dangling chad" of veneer downward to tear it free. By the way, if you're doing four edges of a board, do two opposite edges first, trim the edges, then apply the other two edges.

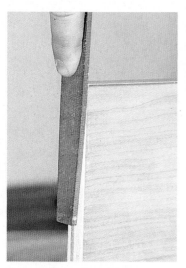

To trim the long edges of the veneer tape, the tool of choice is a mill bastard file. Start by flushing the ends you just broke over, keeping the file flat to the side, and using only a pushing stroke. It should only take a couple strokes to flush up the end.

To trim the tape edges, use the file again, working right to left against the edge. The best method is to start the file at the end of the tape and push lightly against the overhanging edge to start a curl of veneer breaking away from the edge. Continue rolling the curl along the piece, keeping the file angled forward and at a slight bevel to the veneer tape. Once the curl is knocked off, lightly file the bevel again to remove any excess.

The file is too aggressive for a finished edge, so trade it in for some 220-grit sandpaper and finish cleaning up the edge. You'll find some of the adhesive is stuck to the face of the board. This can be lightly sanded off, but proceed carefully to avoid sanding through the face veneer. That's all there is to it, but don't go using the clothes iron, buy your own for the shop!

		european telephone console	**inches**			*european telephone console*	**millimeters**
No.	Item	Dimensions T W L	Material	No.	Item	Dimensions T W L	Material
2	Sides	¾ x 12 x 38	Cherry ply	2	Sides	19 x 305 x 965	Cherry ply
1	Shelf	¾ x 10 x 11	Cherry ply	1	Shelf	19 x 254 x 279	Cherry ply
2	Cleats	¾ x 3 x 11	Cherry ply	2	Cleats	19 x 76 x 279	Cherry ply
1	Kick	¾ x 11 x 7	Cherry ply	1	Kick	19 x 279 x 178	Cherry ply
1	Door	¾ x 11 x 22	Cherry ply	1	Door	19 x 279 x 559	Cherry ply
1	Back	¼ x 11¾ x 25⅝	Cherry ply	1	Back	6 x 298 x 651	Cherry ply
1	Top	⅜ x 11 x 12	Acrylic	1	Top	10 x 279 x 305	Acrylic

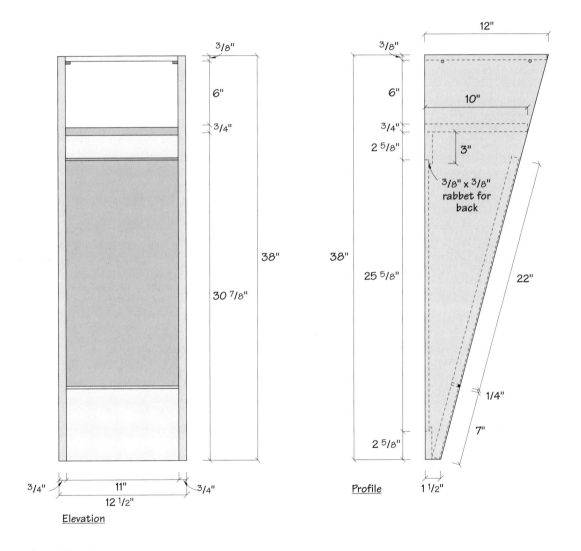

Elevation

Profile

both sides receive iron-on veneer tape, as well as the front edge of the shelf, the top edge of the kick and the top edge of the lower cleat. Don't tape the door edges until the case is assembled. If it's your first time using veneer tape, see the instructions on page 115.

Put It All Together

There are a couple of joinery methods you could use to join the pieces together, but I chose biscuits. Start by marking the location of the shelf on the two sides and cut those biscuit slots. Then mark the location of the upper cleat to biscuit it to the underside of the shelf and into the two sides. The lower cleat is biscuited flush to the back edge and bottom of the sides, while the front kick is flush to the bottom edge, but held in $1/8$" from the front edge to add shadow lines and to keep you from having to align the door perfectly with the edge of the cabinet. With all the biscuit slots cut, sand the inside faces, add some glue and clamp the piece together. Though there's little chance of the piece racking, check it for square.

After the glue is dry, remove the clamps and roll the piece onto its face. Chuck a rabbeting bit into a router and cut a $3/8$" × $3/8$" rabbet in the back edge of the sides and in the top and bottom cleat. Cut a $1/4$" back to fit the space and round the corners to let it drop into place. Don't put the back in yet as it's easier to finish and mount the door hardware with the back off. Go ahead and fit the door, then veneer all four edges.

Finishing Touches: A Clear Top and the Right Hardware

The door is held in place using a continuous hinge mounted to the kick. You should be able to catch six holes in the hinge. Start by mounting the hinge to the kick, then use the two center holes to attach the door. Check to see if the hinge location allows proper clearance. If not, back out your first two screws and use two other holes to maneuver the door one way or the other. When you've got it right, plug the misaligned hinge holes with a toothpick and some

Once the two side wedges are cut to rough size, trim them a little closer to accurate on the jointer. When you're within about $1/16$" of the finished line, clamp the boards together and get out a bench plane. With a little handwork the pieces will match up perfectly.

With all the cross members cut, the biscuit joiner makes it possible to pull the project together. This photo also shows the two cleats in place at the top and bottom of the case.

glue, then redrill the pilot hole and put the screws back in. The door is held in place using a brass lid support and a magnetic catch.

The clear acrylic top is the last construction step, and it's fairly easy to install. Simply drill four shelf pin holes in the sides to allow a $3/8$"-thick piece of acrylic to rest $1/16$" below the top edge. The acrylic is available as a 12" × 12" piece from a number of catalogs as a router-table insert. Cut the piece close to finished size on the table saw, then

sand the piece to a press fit a little at a time. To make the two visible edges presentable, file the edges flat, then sand through 360-grit to a near-perfect edge.

Two coats of clear finish will protect the wood, and the piece is ready to hang. The upper cleat works great as a mounting point using a couple of molleys in the wall. Add a few simple cup hooks to the back side of the door, and you've got a convenient place to hang fold-up umbrellas, keys or any other "near-the-door" items.

shaker
storage cabinet

Maximize storage space in any cabinet
with a couple of simple tricks.

The Shakers always had a knack for packing a lot of storage into a small space and making it look good. The three-sided built-in in the Center family residence at Pleasant Hill, Kentucky, is a prime example. You've probably seen a photo of it. It's the impressive cherry unit that's in an attic with a skylight that illuminates all 45 drawers.

It is in that spirit that I designed this two-door cabinet for a client in Ohio. The family needed to store an enormous number of board games and toys in a relatively small space. The doors had to hide everything.

How to Pack Lots of Stuff Into Small Spaces

Organizing clutter is an interesting problem that you also might face as you design storage in your home or case pieces. Here's what I did: Behind the left door I put a series of five ¾"-thick adjustable solid wood shelves.

These would handle the heavier games and books. Behind the right door is a series of ¼"-thick tempered Masonite shelves. These ten shelves slide in and out of ¼" × ¼" dados.

The Masonite won't hold a lot of weight, but it's just right for storing lightweight objects. Think home office, and you'll know what I mean. Masonite (sometimes called "hardboard") shelves are perfect for storing letterhead, envelopes, CDs and any other paper goods in an office. The other challenge in this piece was getting the shelves, doors and face frame positioned so they didn't interfere with one another. As you'll see in the drawings, it took a few pieces of "blocking" to get everything to work in this cabinet.

Face Frame First

This seems backwards, I know, but begin construction by building the face frame. The size of the case and doors are determined by your face frame, so it's clearly the place to begin.

When ripping out the material for the face frame stiles, cut them each about $\frac{1}{16}$" wider than the dimension called for in the cutting list. This will make your face frame hang over the edge of the case sides. Once the face frame is attached, you can trim it flush for a perfect fit.

I use mortise-and-tenon joinery to build both the face frames and doors. The tenons are $\frac{3}{8}$"-thick and 1" long, and I usually cut a $\frac{3}{8}$" to $\frac{1}{2}$" shoulder on the edges. Be sure to cut your mortises $1\frac{1}{16}$" deep so your tenons don't bottom out. When everything fits, put glue in the mortises, clamp the frame and allow the glue to cure.

Doors Are Second

Next, build the doors. It's much easier to fit the doors into your face frame before it's attached to the case. Build the doors much like you did your face frame by using mortise-and-tenon joints. The only difference is that you need to cut a $\frac{3}{8}$" × $\frac{3}{8}$" groove in the rails and stiles to hold the door panels.

I cut my grooves along the entire length of the stiles; as a result, I cut my tenons with a "haunch" to fill in that extra space on the ends of the stiles. The panels are flat on the front, and beveled on the back side so they fit in the grooves in the rails and stiles. I cut that bevel by setting my table saw blade to 7° and slicing off a little of the back side of each door until the panels

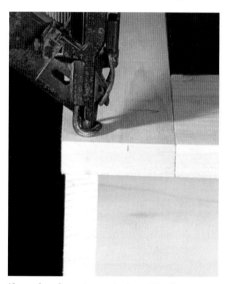

If your face frame is exactly the width of your case, it's going to be difficult to fasten it square. Make life easier by ripping your stiles $\frac{1}{16}$" oversize in width. After you nail and glue the face frame to the case, use a flush-trimming bit in your router to trim the face frame flush with the side of the cabinet's case.

fit snug and without rattling.

Sand the panels up to your final grit (120 will be fine for a painted piece) and assemble the doors. Sand the assembled doors and face frame and then peg the tenons if you like. I used square pegs that I pounded into round holes.

You can see the haunch on the tenons on the rail closest to the camera. When it comes to fitting your panels, remember to work tight in summer and loose in winter. Panels of this size will contract noticeably.

shaker storage cabinet **inches**				
No.	Ltr.	Item	Dimensions T W L	Material
FACE FRAME				
2	A	Stiles	$\frac{3}{4} \times 2\frac{1}{2} \times 51\frac{1}{4}$	Poplar
I	B	Top rail*	$\frac{3}{4} \times 2 \times 45$	Poplar
I	C	Bottom rail*	$\frac{3}{4} \times 5\frac{1}{2} \times 45$	Poplar
DOORS				
4	D	Stiles	$\frac{3}{4} \times 2\frac{1}{2} \times 43\frac{3}{4}$	Poplar
6	E	Rails*	$\frac{3}{4} \times 2\frac{1}{2} \times 18\frac{1}{2}$	Poplar
4	F	Panels	$\frac{5}{8} \times 17 \times 18\frac{5}{8}$	Poplar
CARCASS				
I	G	Top	$\frac{3}{4} \times 19 \times 50$	Maple
2	H	Sides	$\frac{3}{4} \times 17\frac{1}{4} \times 51\frac{1}{4}$	Poplar
I	I	Bottom	$\frac{3}{4} \times 16\frac{3}{4} \times 47$	Poplar
2	J	Dividers	$\frac{3}{4} \times 16\frac{1}{4} \times 45\frac{1}{2}$	Poplar
I	K	Nailing strip	$\frac{3}{4} \times 1\frac{1}{2} \times 6\frac{1}{2}$	Poplar
I	L	Blocking I	$\frac{3}{4} \times 2\frac{1}{4} \times 45\frac{1}{2}$	Poplar
I	M	Blocking 2	$\frac{1}{2} \times 1\frac{3}{4} \times 45\frac{1}{2}$	Poplar
5	N	Adj. shelves	$\frac{3}{4} \times 16\frac{1}{4} \times 22\frac{5}{8}$	Poplar
10	O	Masonite shelves	$\frac{1}{4} \times 16\frac{1}{4} \times 20\frac{1}{4}$	Masonite
I	P	Back	$\frac{1}{2} \times 47 \times 51\frac{1}{4}$	Ply

*= 1" tenon on both ends

shaker storage cabinet **millimeters**				
No.	Ltr.	Item	Dimensions T W L	Material
FACE FRAME				
2	A	Stiles	19 × 64 × 1301	Poplar
I	B	Top rail*	19 × 51 × 1143	Poplar
I	C	Bottom rail*	19 × 140 × 1143	Poplar
DOORS				
4	D	Stiles	19 × 64 × 1111	Poplar
6	E	Rails*	19 × 64 × 470	Poplar
4	F	Panels	16 × 432 × 473	Poplar
CARCASS				
I	G	Top	19 × 483 × 1270	Maple
2	H	Sides	19 × 438 × 1301	Poplar
I	I	Bottom	19 × 425 × 1194	Poplar
2	J	Dividers	19 × 412 × 1156	Poplar
I	K	Nailing strip	19 × 38 × 165	Poplar
I	L	Blocking I	19 × 57 × 1156	Poplar
I	M	Blocking 2	13 × 44 × 1156	Poplar
5	N	Adj. shelves	19 × 412 × 575	Poplar
10	O	Masonite shelves	6 × 412 × 514	Masonite
I	P	Back	13 × 1194 × 1301	Ply

*= 1" tenon on both ends

Top right corner - exploded

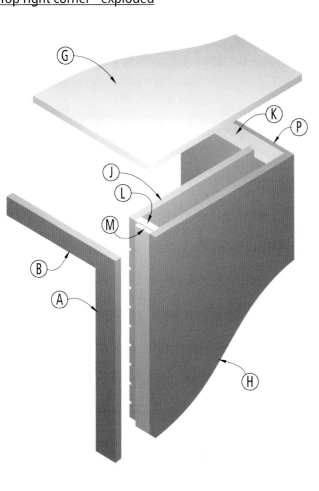

Elevation

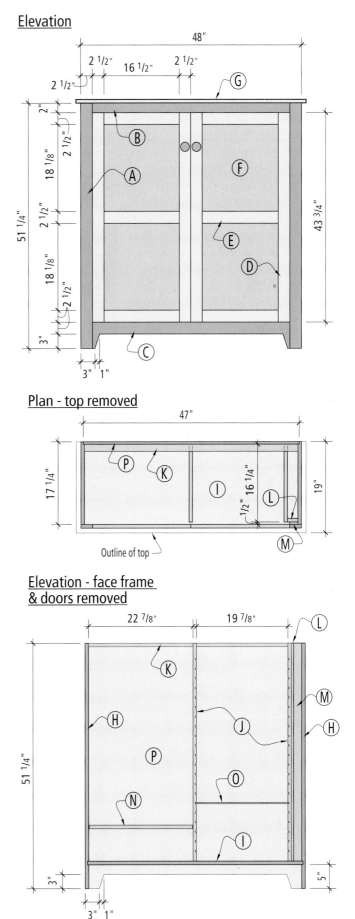

Plan - top removed

Outline of top

Elevation - face frame & doors removed

Finally, the Case

The case goes together quickly thanks to my nail gun. Begin construction by cutting a $^3/_4$"-wide by $^1/_4$"-deep dado in the side pieces for the bottom of the cabinet. I like to use a dado stack in my table saw for this operation. Now cut a $^1/_2$" × $^1/_2$" rabbet on the back edges of the sides to hold the plywood back in place. Sand the inside of the case and get ready for the first bit of assembly.

Put the case together on its back. First put glue in the dados in the sides and fit the bottom in there. Nail the bottom in place from the outside of the case. I use a finish nailer for this task.

Now put the nailing strip in place at the top of the case. The diagrams show you where this needs to be, but essentially it's flush with both the rabbets in the sides and top of the case. Nail it home. Glue and nail the face frame to the case using brads. Trim the face frame flush to the case.

All the Insides

There's nothing complicated about the insides once you have a plan. Begin by cutting the ¼" × ¼" dados in the dividers. These are spaced 2" apart, and there are 21 of them. I used a dado stack in my table saw and simply moved the fence 1¾" after each pass.

Now it's time to add the dividers to the case. Turn the case on its head. Cut a notch in each divider so it will fit around the nailing strip. Get the divider right where it needs to be and nail it in place through the bottom and the nailing strip. Now nail the two blocking pieces, shown on the diagram on page 121, in place. The blocking does a couple things. First, it allows the Masonite shelves to slide in and out without having to swing the doors wide open. Second, the thinner piece of blocking fills in the gap between the divider and face frame, and leaves room for the hinges.

Now drill the holes in the left side of the case and the center divider for the adjustable solid wood shelves. I'm partial to 5mm holes spaced 1⅜" on center.

Mark the base cutouts on the sides, front and plywood back of the case using the diagrams as a guide. Use a jigsaw to make these cuts and clean up your work with sandpaper.

Cut your top to size. I used a piece of bird's-eye maple. You have a couple options for attaching the top. You could use pocket holes, figure-8 fasteners or wooden cleats. No matter which way you go, prepare the case for the top but don't attach it. I like to glue the top to the front edge of the case after finishing.

Finishing

On the knobs, top and all the inside pieces (except the Masonite), I wiped on a light honey-colored stain. Then I painted the case a dark red and added a topcoat of lacquer to protect the paint. Hang the doors, nail in the back and add the knobs.

I have no idea how the Shakers would feel about seeing one of their cabinets filled with "Parcheesi," "Connect Four" and "Uncle Wiggly" games. But I'm sure at least they would approve of the efficient use of space.

You could use a router and a straight bit to make this cut as long as you had a reliable way of guiding the router (such as an edge guide). I find a table saw is much faster for this operation.

In addition to cutting the detail on the sides and front (above), I also cut it on the bottom of the plywood back, which gives it a finished look when the cabinet is viewed from down low or from a distance.

Once you nail the dividers in place through the bottom piece, turn the case over on its feet and nail through the nailing strip into the dividers (left).

Supplies

Woodworker's Supply • 800-645-9292
Amerock non-mortising hinges - #891-749

Horton Brasses Inc. • 800-754-9127,
or www.horton-brasses.com
1½"-diameter maple knobs - #WK-3

apothecary **cabinet**

This cabinet packs lots of drawers into a
small space, making it the perfect place to
store all of your small valuables.

I like cabinets with lots of drawers, especially apothecary cabinets. When planning this project, I took a short trip on the Internet and downloaded a variety of pictures and plans for apothecary style cabinets, then used those pictures as a starting point for the design.

The cabinet body is based on a square, with the legs lifting it up for a more vertical look. I started with square drawer fronts, putting four across and four down, but didn't like the repetition of sixteen squares. I tried various combinations — rows with two drawers, three drawers and four drawers; I decided on two rows of four drawers, one row of three drawers and one row of two drawers. This gives the cabinet visual balance.

I liked the contrasting dark drawer fronts with the lighter wood of the cabinet and legs, and was lucky to find a great piece of walnut to use for the drawer fronts. I waited until the cabi-net was completed before selecting the hardware, then took a couple of the drawers with me to my local home improvement center to pick out the knobs. This helped me find just the right look to finish the cabinet.

Make the Parts

Begin by cutting out all the parts as shown in the Materials List. Remember to cut parts B, C, D and E to allow for the hardwood edging to be added. Glue the hardwood edges on parts B, D and E. The edging will be glued on the top and bottom panels C after the rabbets are cut into the back edges of these panels.

Lay out the sides and cut the biscuit slots for the shelves using a straight-edge as a guide for the biscuit joiner. Next, cut the slots into the ends of the shelves. Take your time and carefully lay out the dividers; when these are glued into place they will function as the drawer guides. Now lay out and cut the slots into the tops and bottoms of

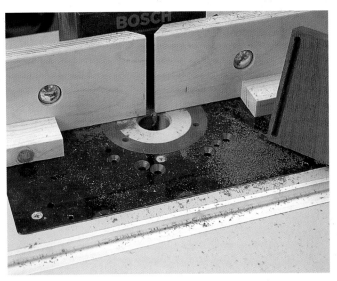

Rough-cut the bevels on the legs with the band saw, then smooth them with a belt sander or block plane.

Cut stopped dadoes in the drawer fronts using a table-mounted router.

the shelves for the vertical dividers. Mark each shelf as top, middle and bottom so you can keep the shelves and dividers in proper orientation during assembly.

Align the Top and Bottom

Dry assemble the sides, shelves and dividers. On a flat work surface, lay this assembly on its front edge on $^3/_8$"-tall spacers. Stand the top and bottom panels on their front edges directly on the work surface and put them in proper alignment with the shelf assembly. Mark where the sides meet the top and bottom panels, then lay out and cut the biscuit slots in the top and bottom panels, and cut the matching biscuit slots into the top and bottom ends of the sides.

Cut the Rabbets for the Back Panel

Once again, dry assemble the sides, shelves, dividers and top and bottom parts. Lay this entire assembly on its face, using the $^3/_8$" spacers to support the shelf assembly. Make sure the top and bottom panels rest directly on the work surface. The back edges of the top, bottom and side panel should all be flush. The dividers' and shelves' back edges should all be $^1/_2$" below these edges. This last dry assembly step just helps you see how this cabinet fits together — if you feel confident

in all you've done so far, go ahead and cut the rabbets in the panels. Cut all of the rabbets $^1/_2$" × $^1/_2$" — the full length of the parts.

Now glue the hardwood edges to the ends and fronts of the top and bottom panels. Remember to create miter joints on the two outside corners of these panels.

Shape the Edges

Tilt your table saw blade to a 30° angle and cut a bevel on the front and ends of the false top. Use a $^3/_8$" roundover router bit and cut the bullnose profile on the bottom panel. On the top panel, round over only the bottom of the edge. A router set up in a router table is the easiest and safest way to do this.

Build the Base

Cut the foot bevel on two adjacent sides of each leg. This can be done safely in two steps: After drawing the bevels on the legs, rough-cut the bevel using a band saw or jigsaw. Then use a belt sander or block plane to complete the bevel cuts to the lines.

Next lay out the arches on the front, back and side rails. This can be easily done by marking the center of each rail, then making a cross $1^1/_2$" from the top edge of the rails on the center mark. Hold the ends of a thin strip of wood on the two bottom corners of each rail and bend the strip until it

By capturing the drawer sides between the front and back parts, the drawers can be assembled quickly using just two clamps.

touches the $1^1/_2$" mark. Using a pencil, have an assistant draw the arch on the rail, then cut the arch with a band saw or jigsaw up to the pencil mark. Use a curved sanding block, a sanding drum chucked in a drill press or an oscillating spindle sander to smooth the arches.

Lay out and cut the biscuit slots in the ends of the rails and in the top edges of the legs. Use two biscuits placed side by side and spaced about $^1/_8$" to $^3/_{16}$" apart.

Final Sanding and Finishing

After your final sanding of all the parts, mask off the biscuit slots with tape and apply finish. You'll find that finishing all of the parts prior to assembly is easier than trying to apply finish in all the nooks and crannies of the small drawer

apothecary cabinet **inches**

No.	Ltr.	Item	Dimensions T W L	Material	Comments
1	A	False top	3/4 x 14 x 21 3/4	Ash	
2	B	Sides	3/4 x 13 x 18 1/4	Ash Plywd	FS: includes 3/8 x 3/4 ash hardwood front edges
2	C	Top & bottom	3/4 x 13 3/8 x 20 1/2	Ash Plywd	FS: includes 3/8 x 3/4 ash hardwood front & side edges
3	D	Shelves	3/4 x 12 1/2 x 18 1/4	Ash Plywd	FS: includes 3/8 x 3/4 ash hardwood front edges
9	E	Dividers	3/4 x 12 1/2 x 4	Ash Plywd	FS: includes 3/8 x 3/4 ash hardwood front edges
1	F	Back	1/2 x 19 1/4 x 17 3/4	Birch Plywd	
4	G	Legs	1 1/2 x 1 1/2 x 6 1/2	Ash	
2	H	Front/back base rails	3/4 x 2 x 16 3/4	Ash	
2	J	Side base rails	3/4 x 2 x 10	Ash	
8	K	Drawer fronts	3/4 x 4 x 4	Walnut	
2	L	Drawer fronts	3/4 x 5 1/4 x 4	Walnut	
1	M	Drawer front	3/4 x 6 1/4 x 4	Walnut	
2	N	Drawer fronts	3/4 x 8 3/4 x 4	Walnut	
26	P	Drawer sides	1/2 x 4 high x 11 1/8	Poplar	
8	Q	Drawer backs	1/2 x 4 x 3 1/2 high	Poplar	
2	R	Drawer backs	1/2 x 5 1/4 x 3 1/2 high	Poplar	
1	S	Drawer back	1/2 x 6 1/4 x 3 1/2 high	Poplar	
2	T	Drawer backs	1/2 x 5 1/4 x 3 1/2 high	Poplar	
8	U	Drawer bottoms	1/4 x 3 1/2 x 12 1/8	Luan Plywd	
2	V	Drawer backs	1/4 x 4 3/4 x 12 1/8	Luan Plywd	
1	W	Drawer bottom	1/4 x 5 3/4 x 12 1/8	Luan Plywd	
2	X	Drawer bottoms	1/4 x 5 3/4 x 12 1/8	Luan Plywd	

FS=Finished size

HARDWARE: 13 knobs and 2 knob plates

apothecary cabinet **millimeters**

No.	Ltr.	Item	Dimensions T W L	Material	Comments
1	A	False top	19 x 356 x 552	Ash	
2	B	Sides	19 x 330 x 463	Ash Plywd	FS: includes 10 x 19 ash hardwood front edges
2	C	Top & bottom	19 x 340 x 521	Ash Plywd	FS: includes 10 x 19 ash hardwood front edges
3	D	Shelves	19 x 318 x 463	Ash Plywd	FS: includes 10 x 19 ash hardwood front & side edges
9	E	Dividers	19 x 318 x 102	Ash Plywd	FS: includes 10 x 19 ash hardwood front edges
1	F	Back	13 x 489 x 451	Birch Plywd	
4	G	Legs	38 x 38 x 165	Ash	
2	H	Front/back base rails	19 x 51 x 425	Ash	
2	J	Side base rails	19 x 51 x 254	Ash	
8	K	Drawer fronts	19 x 102 x 102	Walnut	
2	L	Drawer fronts	19 x 133 x 102	Walnut	
1	M	Drawer front	19 x 158 x 102	Walnut	
2	N	Drawer fronts	19 x 222 x 102	Walnut	
26	P	Drawer sides	13 x 102 high x 282	Poplar	
8	Q	Drawer backs	13 x 102 x 89 high	Poplar	
2	R	Drawer backs	13 x 133 x 89 high	Poplar	
1	S	Drawer back	13 x 158 x 89 high	Poplar	
2	T	Drawer backs	13 x 222 x 89 high	Poplar	
8	U	Drawer bottoms	6 x 89 x 308	Luan Plywd	
2	V	Drawer backs	6 x 121 x 308	Luan Plywd	
1	W	Drawer bottom	6 x 146 x 308	Luan Plywd	
2	X	Drawer bottoms	6 x 209 x 308	Luan Plywd	

FS=Finished size

HARDWARE: 13 knobs and 2 knob plates

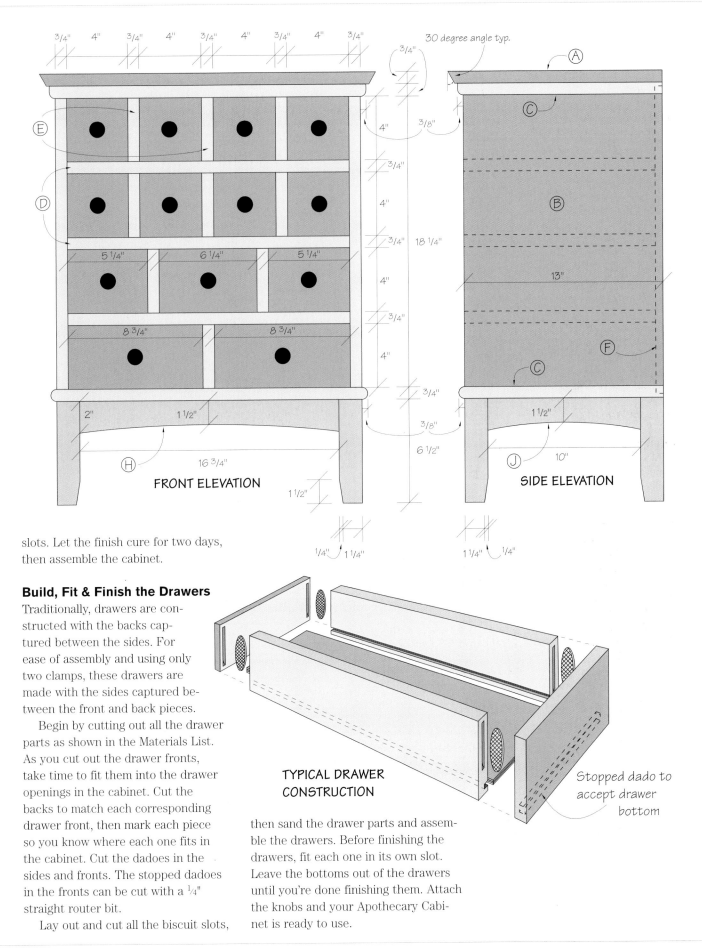

FRONT ELEVATION

SIDE ELEVATION

slots. Let the finish cure for two days, then assemble the cabinet.

Build, Fit & Finish the Drawers

Traditionally, drawers are constructed with the backs captured between the sides. For ease of assembly and using only two clamps, these drawers are made with the sides captured between the front and back pieces.

Begin by cutting out all the drawer parts as shown in the Materials List. As you cut out the drawer fronts, take time to fit them into the drawer openings in the cabinet. Cut the backs to match each corresponding drawer front, then mark each piece so you know where each one fits in the cabinet. Cut the dadoes in the sides and fronts. The stopped dadoes in the fronts can be cut with a ¼" straight router bit.

Lay out and cut all the biscuit slots,

TYPICAL DRAWER
CONSTRUCTION

Stopped dado to accept drawer bottom

then sand the drawer parts and assemble the drawers. Before finishing the drawers, fit each one in its own slot. Leave the bottoms out of the drawers until you're done finishing them. Attach the knobs and your Apothecary Cabinet is ready to use.

index